Fifty Years of Freedom

Fifty Years of Freedom

Researched and written by
Rob Batiste, Pete Burnard, Jon Crocker, Dave Edmonds,
James Falla, Kay Leslie, John Neale, Nick Mollet, Mark Ogier,
Edwin Parks, Michaela Wakeford and Fiona White.

Pictures collected by
Geoff Brehaut, Chris George and Brian Green.

Edited by
Nick Machon.

gp

The Guernsey Press Co. Ltd
1995

© The Guernsey Press Co. Ltd.

All rights reserved. No part of this publication may be reproduced, stored in a retrieval system, or transmitted in any form or by any means, electronic, mechanical, photocopying, recording or otherwise, without the prior permission of The Guernsey Press Co. Ltd.

First published 1995

Made and printed in **Great Britain** by
The Guernsey Press Co. Ltd, Guernsey, Channel Islands.

ISBN 0 902550 57 8

Introduction

Fifty Years of Freedom outlines the events and major changes to this community in the years since the Occupation ended.

In pictures and words it traces the big influx of people returning after the war, some who left as children and came back as young adults, new husbands and wives seen for the first time by islanders who did not evacuate, the resumption of pre-war lives or starting from scratch, the altering face of Guernsey over five decades and the change in attitudes from the more formal and deferential early years to the more relaxed but less cohesive population we have today.

Through all this there are the shipwrecks, air disasters, car crashes, daring rescues, births, deaths and marriages.

There are glimpses of people who were to make it into the headlines in later years and there are the annual events such as the Battle of Flowers, Muratti and Liberation celebrations.

Each page also has snippets from the outside world to help place events in their context - many people recall with great clarity what they were doing at the time of the Cuban missile crisis, the Profumo scandal, the Kennedy assassination, John Lennon being shot.

There is food rationing, the growth of rescue services, pop music and the swinging sixties, oil spills at sea, a tunnel under the sea to ease the sewage problem, leisure activities and industries.

And there is constitutional reform, European unity, some massive developments and the growth of the finance industry.

Most of all this is a celebration of the people of the bailiwick and how they adapted in the decades since the Occupation.

The information and pictures came from within the resources of the Guernsey Evening Press, and many of the earlier photographs are reproductions from the newspapers of the day.

Fifty Years of Freedom does not set out to be a definitive history of the island, though readers will find most of the major and many of the minor happenings recorded within these pages.

First atom bomb tested in New Mexico.
Street parties in Britain mark VE Day. Allied
victors carve up post-war Europe.

1945

Guernsey's airport was once again open for civilian passengers by mid-July. In those balmy days the Evening Press not only published the number of flights arriving each day but a list of the passengers as well.

JERSEY AIRWAYS *Flying Again!* and **GUERNSEY AIRWAYS**
FREQUENT DAILY SERVICES
LONDON – GUERNSEY – JERSEY
Apply 10, SMITH STREET, ST. PETER-PORT. TEL.

Jersey and Guernsey Airways were back in business, offering frequent daily services to London and Jersey.

Fruit was exported by air for the first time. Nearly 1,000lb of choice fruit was despatched in a De Havilland Dominie flown by Captain S. T. Cripps of Guernsey Airways.

1945

Art treasures looted by Nazis found in an Austrian mine shaft. US bomber crashes into Empire State Building in New York.

On 7 June 1945 King George VI and Queen Elizabeth arrived in Guernsey for a short visit. They arrived by air from Jersey, escorted by a squadron of Mustang fighters, and were greeted by a salute fired using a battery of captured German guns. After touring the island the royal couple arrived at Candie Gardens where a huge crowd had gathered to see them. The Bailiff, Victor Carey, read the loyal address. The King and Queen left the same evening by air.

There was still much German hardware lying about and islanders were being warned not to touch anything they found, especially mines like the one below.

US drops atom bomb on Hiroshima, 6 August, killing 140,000. Three days later Nagasaki destroyed by second bomb.

1945

October saw the announcement of the award of the Military Cross to two local men, Hubert Nicolle (below) and James Symes (above), for their part in a daring 1940 reconnaissance trip to occupied Guernsey. Unfortunately the two were unable to return to the UK and were forced to surrender to the Germans.

The first large parties of evacuees returned to the island in October aboard the Isle of Jersey after five years of exile.

1945

Pierre Laval, French Vichy Government leader, executed, as is Vidkun Quisling, leader of Norwegian puppet government.

In December the Alderney exiles were at last able to go home after the island had been sufficiently cleared of the mess left behind by the Germans (above). Returning islanders were sternly warned not to fraternise with the remaining POWs.

Local Newspapers

The local newspapers will, commencing from Monday next, each be published three times a fortnight.

Publication will be in the following sequence:

Next week:—
 Monday, "Press."
 Wednesday, "Star."
 Saturday, "Press."

Week commencing April 16:
 Monday, "Star."
 Wednesday, "Press."
 Saturday, "Star,"
and so on in that order.

Printing of newspapers soon resumed, but not daily due to newsprint shortages.

Luxury goods were in short supply long after the islands had been liberated. But soon advertisements promising a taste of future treats were appearing (right).

FRY'S CHOCOLATE CREAM

The delicious cream centre gives you EXTRA ENERGY

OF the good things to which you can now look forward not the least is an occasional bar of Fry's delicious Chocolate Cream. Supplies, we hope, will soon be on their way. Not as much as we'd *like* to send, but as much as we can.

League of Nations is replaced by United Nations. Antibiotic streptomycin promises an end to TB.

1946

The first Liberation Day Cavalcade was held on 9 May. The winning float was Our Liberators, entered by a Mr Guilliard, with a host of children representing the armed and caring services.

A huge crowd turned out to watch the parade, which was led by the Royal Marine band from the battleship HMS King George V. There was also a flypast by squadrons of the RAF.

1946

Bank of England passes into public ownership. National Health Service announced in UK. First bikini goes on show in Paris.

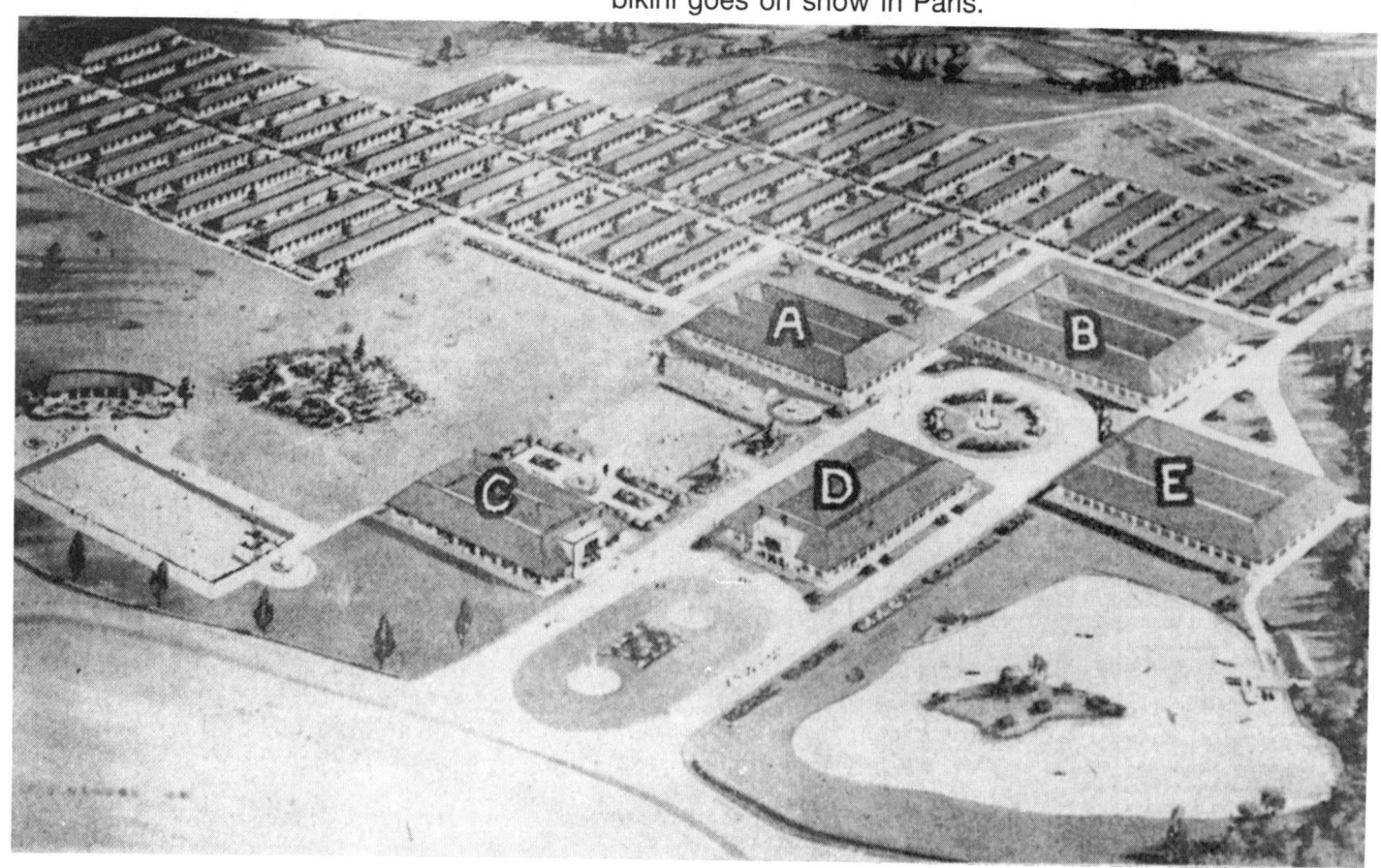

Plans for the building of a huge Butlin's Holiday Camp on L'Eree were rejected by the States in November. The States debated the matter for three hours but eventually voted against the idea by 35 votes to 13.

Herm was uninhabited except for the caretaker, Mr A. Prior, his wife and dog Rex (bottom left). The States were being urged to buy the island as a 'simple playground' for islanders. The price was £15,000.

Italy becomes a republic. Pilot sees nine UFOs over Washington. Bread rationing in Britain after a poor harvest.

1946

The bulk of the liberating troops of Force 135 left the island in July aboard the Empire Peacemaker amid emotional scenes. Many of them promised that they would be back as soon as they could manage it.

Some Liberators found it very difficult to tear themselves away from their new found Guernsey friends. This Royal Army Service Corps soldier is certainly making the most of his last few minutes in Guernsey.

12,000 people attended the 1946 Battle of Flowers, the first since the war. Commentators said that the number of entries was not up to pre-war standards but that the quality was as good as ever. In those days the exhibits were stripped by the crowd who indulged in a real battle of flowers, pelting each other with blooms after the judging was over.

1946

King David Hotel, Jerusalem, is bombed - 91 die. First Biro goes on sale. Railways in Britain to be nationalised.

Inspector Sculpher (above), who had commanded the island's police force during the early period of the Occupation, was sacked in February 1946. He was blamed for a breakdown in discipline which allowed members of the force to steal food from German stores. He was among those deported to Germany but was reinstated as chief officer after the Liberation. He appealed against his dismissal and was reinstated before finally retiring.

December gales battered a huge hole in the Alderney Breakwater (left). The damage was described as the worst in living memory and the worst breach was 40 yards long below water. Breakwater repairs were then paid for by the British taxpayer.

The ancient feudal court of the Fiefs d'Anneville and de Fauville (below) sat in October, reviving an ancient tradition dating back to Norman times.

American gangster Al Capone dies. Big freeze blacks out much of Britain.

1947

Early 1947 saw the completion of a nine-year project to build the 123,000 tons dam in St Saviour's. Work began in August 1938 but had to be suspended in June 1940 following the Occupation. The Germans left the dam virtually untouched and it was opened early in the year.

12   **1947**   President Truman launches the Cold War by warning of the threat posed by communism.

The heaviest snow for many years fell on the last weekend of January. Drifts were two feet deep in the higher parishes. Above is the view down St Julian's Avenue; youngsters toboggan and make a giant snowball (left), while Tom and Peggy (below) who were born in India, get their first taste of snow.

Lord Louis Mountbatten becomes India's last viceroy. Europe accepts the Marshall Aid Plan to rebuild after the war.

1947

War hero 'Monty' – Field Marshal The Viscount Montgomery of Alamein KG GCB DSO (left) – provided islanders with the biggest thrill since the Liberation on a short visit to the island in May. He made two speeches, and praised the local men who had fought in the war and the islanders' fortitude through the Occupation.

A troupe of visiting variety artistes made an unscheduled stop in France on their way to perform in Guernsey in January (right). The Aerovan plane was caught in a thick rain storm on its way from Southampton to Guernsey and ended up making a forced landing on to a French beach. The troupe eventually reached the island two days later.

These pupils (left) from St Andrew's School were among youngsters called in to help in the search for the dangerous pest the Colorado beetle, following unconfirmed reports of its presence in the island in June. Anybody finding the beetle stood to claim a £10 reward.

1947

Pakistan gains independence from India. Chuck Yeager smashes the sound barrier in a Bell X-1.

The way they were. The Salvation Army organised a day out for these old folk, all of whom were aged over 80.

The Southern Railway steamer Falaise made its maiden voyage in July 1947. Its presence on the Southampton to St Malo route re-opened the service which had been suspended. Initially the mailboat called at the islands on weekends. British-built, it carried 1,400 passengers.

A piece of history lost. This tree was thought to be nearly 300 years old, was 100 feet high and weighed nearly 20 tons. Situated in a field at the rear of Les Vauxbelets, it had to be cut down because the Germans had killed the tree at the roots.

Until the days of Matt Le Tissier, Len Duquemin was the island's best known professional footballer. In August 1947 he made his professional debut for Tottenham Hotspur against Sheffield Wednesday in a League Division Two fixture. Spurs won 5-1.

Burma leaves the Commonwealth. London Co-Op opens the first British supermarket. Mahatma Gandhi gunned down in India.

1948

Constitutional reform was in the air and on 17 January UK Home Secretary Chuter Ede visited the island for a 'conference on reform' with the Bailiff and jurats. During his visit the Evening Press highlighted the island's population problem with the headline: 'People arrive at rate of 70 each week.' The following week it was revealed that all newcomers would need licences to occupy homes here.

The last sitting of the old style States with jurats on the top bench. Reform had been agreed and the next general election would see the introduction of conseillers and the demise of voting jurats. The Royal Court was reconstructed after this picture was taken to accommodate the reformed House.

DR. GIBSON HEADS THE TOWN POLL

December 29 and the Evening Press records the first election under the new constitution. There was a very low turn-out. In Town, just 2,974 of the 11,360 on the electoral roll bothered to vote. 'Another surprise was the failure of the Guernsey Labour Group of 11 candidates to impress the voters,' the report records. Only one of the candidates, J. R. D. Jones, was elected. Communist candidate Bill Balshaw won just 27 votes in the Vale.

1948

Ceylon gains independence. Communists take over Prague. Thor Heyerdahl crosses Pacific Ocean on the raft Kon-Tiki.

Sark's new harbour at La Maseline, started before the Occupation, was completed just 10 years after the first stone was laid. Some 25,000 tons of granite were quarried from Sark and the final cost of the harbour was £50,000.

Sark hit the headlines on February 28, thanks to a visit from Field Marshal Montgomery of Alamein (above). He posed with the schoolchildren and then, to their delight, asked for – and got them – a whole day off. As he left the island he said, with real enthusiasm: 'What a wonderful place it is.'

Complete with his world-famous beret, Field Marshal Montgomery returned to Guernsey for the second time at the end of his stay in the bailiwick (left). He was greeted by (left to right): Edric Lucas, British Railways agent, Lt-Governor Sir Philip Neame and his aide de camp, Captain Michael Mellish.

Russians blockade Berlin, massive airlift by West to feed the city. US tests plutonium bomb at Eniwatok Atoll, Marshall Islands.

1948

17

The Liberation Day celebrations were marked by the presence of Guernsey's own VC, Major Wallace Le Patourel, who was officially welcomed home to his island. French and Royal Navy sailors took part in the huge cavalcade which marked the third anniversary of freedom.

A 120-ton, 50ft Russian gun from the Mirus Battery is cut up for scrap. The 15 inch barrel, which could propel one ton shells 20 miles or more, is cut down the middle before being further sectioned.

1948

State of Israel formed amid civil war pitting Arabs against Jews. 'Reds under the beds' in US as McCarthy hearings open.

The queue for Muratti tickets started at 1.30pm the day before the match, but even early arrivals were disappointed as there were only 34 pavilion tickets on sale at Collins Boot Stores. Open stand and chair tickets also sold out quickly and on match day officials were hoping that a further 200 tickets would be sent on from Jersey.

Some familiar faces among the GIAAC team selected for the inter-insular (right). From the left, back row, are: V. G. Collenette; M. J. Rayson; J. W. de Putron; J. F. Adams. Front row: R. C. Priest; B. F. L. Pontin; R. A. Davidson; F. Mellanby and F. Carre.

The year 1948 was welcomed in with dance as islanders crowded the hotel dance floors to ring in the new. More than 700 packed the Royal Hotel to bring in 'A happier and brighter New Year', while more than 1,000 celebrated at St George's Hall. The Evening Press reported that the island's agricultural and horticultural societies, after 'the glorious summer of 1947', all agreed to hold shows again in 1948 and there was talk in the west about holding La Chevauchee de St Michel, 'an old processional custom which has long since died out'.

Even though the war had been over for three years, food was in short supply. In 1947 the Bailiff, Sir Ambrose Sherwill, appealed to islanders to produce as many vegetables as possible and the appeal worked. These potato gatherers at Le Preel, Castel, were playing their part in creating what was expected to be an island surplus of 900 tons of spuds. The tomato industry was booming with seven-and-a-half million trays being exported.

Vinyl records go on sale in the United States. Mao's peasant army marches on Peking. NATO is formed.

1949

The 121 elms which lined St Julian's Avenue were felled during the early days of January by a team of 25 men working for contractor Jack Hodder. The trees took eight days to fell and clear up and they were replaced by Norwegian maples.

The Home Secretary, Mr J. Chuter Ede, was in Alderney in February for the swearing in of the island's first post-war States. He was met on his arrival by the Lt-Governor, Sir Philip Neame.

1949

Laurence Olivier's Hamlet sweeps the Oscars at the awards ceremony. Food rationing ends in Britain.

The marriage of 25-year-old Joan Tostevin in February was unusual as she was the first local woman to marry a member of the German forces which occupied the island. Hugo Rutsch, a 37-year-old printer by trade, was given special dispensation by the Lt-Governor, Sir Philip Neame, to return to the island for four weeks to get married. The newly-wed Rutschs went to live in Gloucestershire where Hugo was an agricultural worker.

It was announced in July that Yorkshireman Major Peter Wood was to be the new tenant of Herm.

Stone exports resumed in January after a nine-year gap due to the Occupation when A. and F. Manuelle sent a cargo to Dover on board the Channel Coast.

Maiden flight of the Comet jet airliner. Berlin airlift stops as Russians end their blockade of the city.

1949

One of the sporting highlights of the year was the summer visit of the Burtonwood Gadgets, the baseball team from the American base. They played a series of matches at Beau Sejour in front of crowds as big as 3,000 and went through the series unbeaten.

Guernsey suffered its worst drought to date with streamflow all but drying up and growers facing major problems. The crisis was highlighted first in April and by July, restrictions were in force. Growers' water was rationed, but 700 of them lost their supply altogether for exceeding their quota.

The golf course opened for play on L'Ancresse Common.

1949

'Acid bath' murderer John Haig is hanged.
Hawaii becomes the 50th state of the union.

Islanders turned out in their thousands for the visit of Princess Elizabeth and Prince Philip to Guernsey in June. The royal couple spent a day in Alderney before coming to Guernsey where they visited the hospital named after the princess. They also visited Saumarez Park and saw examples of the island's thriving agricultural and horticultural industries.

The start of one of Britain's premier pigeon races from the end of the White Rock. The race was organised by the News of the World.

US senator John McCarthy's communist witch-hunt puts Hollywood people in the spotlight. India becomes a republic.

1950

The Turkish freighter Edirne lies stricken on a reef off Burhou Island, abandoned by her crew. The Edirne refloated on the high tide, only to sink in 15-20 fathoms of water two miles north-west of Quesnard Lighthouse. In one of the biggest rescues carried out by the Guernsey lifeboat Queen Victoria, 50 crew were taken off the freighter and taken to St Peter Port. The Edirne was on passage from Gibraltar to Denmark with a cargo of cattle food. No lives were lost.

Early morning call: In the early hours of 4 July, 1950, the Ward family at Le Picquerel were woken by a particularly violent thunderstorm and a meteorite! When Mr Ward left for work he discovered a hole 3ft by 2ft in diameter and 5ft deep outside house.

1950

Atom spy Klaus Fuchs is found guilty of spying for Russia.

Saturday afternoon and a hunting they would go, well these four young men of L'Ancresse did in the summer of 1950. S. Martin, E. Bean, P. Bean and E. Le Huray liked to spend their spare time octopus hunting in Miellette Bay, south of Fort Doyle. Armed only with 3ft long hooks the four lads caught as many as 82 on this particular low tide, some measuring between 2 and 3ft across. On occasions, however, the lads caught the multi-legged creatures as big as 6ft across.

Catch in a million: Capt. Hubert Petit shows off the 6ft long, 93lb sturgeon caught off Pleinmont before it is shipped to Billingsgate fish market. It was thought to be the first sturgeon caught off Guernsey. By tradition the first sturgeon caught each year has to go to the monarch. It is a highly valuable fish as it yields caviar and isinglass.

French troops clash with communist guerillas in Vietnam.

1950

End of a bomb. Three days before Guy Fawkes' Night, 1950, a 650lb German mine found off Spur Point, St Sampson's, is destroyed. Top left – Chief Petty Officer W. Pitt removes the lethal detonators; top right – Inspector F. Le Cocq has a hand in pulling out the mine's charge; Bottom left – the explosive burning in the mine sends out a vivid glare; bottom right – the shell of the mine is all that remains after the 650lb of explosives have been destroyed.

The Royal Hotel was crowded out as film starlet Petula Clark (left) gave a performance at a ball to raise funds for the Guernsey Boy Scouts' Association.

Lt-Governor Sir Philip Neame had his term of office extended.

1950

First kidney transplant in Chicago. Korean War starts. Charles M. Schulz creates Charlie Brown.

Five years after the end of the Second World War and German schoolchildren tuck into a midday meal, some of which contained Guernsey tomatoes sent by the Guernsey people. In 1949 Guernsey's surplus tomatoes were canned and sent to needy families in Germany.

Another big step in the saving of life and limb: county officer R. H. Blanchford of St John Ambulance and Mr R. Lihou, a radio control expert, are seen during an exercise off the east of Sark to test a new scheme which ensures complete radio control coverage of the sea area around Guernsey.

Thankfully no one was hurt when this Pickford Aviation Aerovan crashed on its approach to Guernsey Airport after a wheel steadfastly refused to lower. The plane, on its way from Cherbourg, was carrying six passengers.

Atom bomb testing moves to Nevada. Last of the Nazi war criminals tried at Nuremburg is hanged.

1951

The first visit of a 'hover plane' was enthusiastically reported in October. A Sikorsky helicopter from the Royal Navy station at Gosport arrived as part of an exercise. The Lt-Governor and Bailiff greeted the Alvis Leonides-powered aircraft. Sir Philip's enthusiasm was such that he climbed aboard for a flight to the Castle Emplacement. Plans to fly to Sark had to be scrapped after that island decided their cattle 'might be panicked' by the low-flying machine.

A Town policy of banning traffic from some streets, except by permit, was introduced and reportedly caused chaos. Traffic piled up at Smith Street as motorists were forced to try to turn or reverse, having apparently forgotten about the new 'no road' system.

1951

Festival of Britain opens in London. Worst floods in US history leave 200,000 homeless in Kansas and Missouri.

The approach to Castle Cornet began to take on its now familiar arched shape as the old wooden walk was replaced with new girders. On January 24th these photographs showed the first arch in position on the bridge. The work was done by Messrs E. Farley and Son of Jersey. The bridge made tragic news later in the year when a local man fell to his death from it.

Five French fishing boats which sought shelter in St Peter Port Harbour in May prepare to sail.

The Mau Mau uprising starts in Kenya as white settlers are murdered.

1951

Appointment with Venus, the big screen production which involved hundreds of islanders as extras, was an artistic highpoint during the year. Barry Jones, who moved from the Rohais to develop his unique property at Le Catioroc, played a large part in the production of the film. He was pictured 'enjoying a brief holiday' with Maurice Colbourne just before they started to make the film and were reported to be 'praying for fine weather'.

Jones made the headlines again a few months later when he decided to have the names of the year's victorious Muratti team inscribed for posterity on a specially made weather vane. The feline instrument, based on the Guernsey lions, was erected at Le Catioroc. The Muratti attracted a record crowd of 12,692. They watched 'a thrilling game' in which Guernsey and Jersey failed to score until the local side put two balls into the net during extra time.

1951

US sets up Greenham Common air base in Berkshire. Libya declares independence.

A dramatic explosion, described as the worst in the history of the Guernsey Gas Light Company, ripped through their Bouet premises on 4 April. A faulty exhaust system was thought to be responsible for the explosion in the boiler house. Three employees were badly hurt. The boiler house was torn apart and windows in the office were shattered. The explosion also broke windows in houses at the Bouet.

An innovative plan to highlight, literally, one of the most popular tourist attractions, was completed in September. The Little Chapel was 'tastefully' lit after Mr A. Foard, of Sunnycroft, Mont Saint, constructed a plan which enabled people to put a sixpenny coin in a slot machine to turn on the lights.

Selection of scenes from the big Liberation Cavalcade.

Pope Pius XII declares television a threat to family life. Death of King George VI.

1952

The year began with an event that affected not only the lives of every resident of the Bailiwick, but also every resident of the British Commonwealth - the death of King George VI and the accession of Queen Elizabeth II. Islanders learned the sad news of the King's death in the Evening Press of 6 February: "The King passes peacefully away" read the headline. Two days later, Elizabeth was proclaimed Queen in London, but while the Press again gave the news front page prominence, the story was tempered by a report of the air of mourning around St Peter Port, with flags flying at half mast and many shops displaying mourning bands. Guernsey proclaimed the new monarch the following day, with a ceremony in the Royal Court. Following the official business in the courthouse, the proclamation was read to the crowds outside the building and in Market Square, which was packed with schoolchildren, their parents, States members and members of the island's emergency services.

One local firm of growers had a major honour conferred upon it in March when it became the first nursery to be asked to exhibit flowers at the prestigious Royal Horticultural Society's Show, being held at Westminster. Caledonia Nurseries sent a total of 54 varieties of camellia to London, where they were exhibited alongside camellias from as far afield as the USA. The display was described as "the most comprehensive display of named camellias ever staged", and nothing like it had been attempted in Britain before. Small wonder that the news of Caledonia Nurseries success made the front page, including a photo of two of the company's staff carefully packing the chosen blooms.

1952

Britain now has the atom bomb, following America and Russia.

Passengers bound for Sark had to find alternative transport when the Island Commodore sank in St Peter Port Harbour early in the morning of 25 June. The cause was unclear. Salvage work did not begin immediately, and while talks about how best to go about raising the sunken vessel started, the sight of the boat under water became something of an attraction among locals. Scores of people made their way to number 5 berth to watch as workmen salvaged various bits of equipment prior to the lifting operation proper getting under way. At low tide the boat could be seen clearly, but even then there was no sign of damage. The Commodore was finally raised on 3 July.

The march of technology finally caught up with Sark in June, when the island's telecommunications link with Guernsey was given a major boost. Fittingly, it was La Dame de Serk, Dame Sybil Hathaway, who was the first to try the new radio telephone system and called the Bailiff, Sir Ambrose Sherwill. Once the link was established, representatives of Guernsey's Telephone Council entertained at Stock's Hotel. Sark had had three telephones during the First World War, and none at all during the Second. But the quality of the cable link between the island and Guernsey was not good, and prompted the Guernsey Telephone Council to install the radio connection.

The Soviet Union test launches its first intercontinental ballistic missile.

1952

The Bailiwick finally got its marine ambulance in July, when the Flying Christine was launched with due ceremony by the Dean, the Very Rev. E. L. Frossard. Although a far cry from the purpose-built marine ambulance of today, the boat was nonetheless seen as a great boon to the St John Ambulance and Rescue Service. It had been converted by the Guernsey Yacht Yard (a task that took six weeks), and had been bought for the service with money raised by the local branch of the Round Table. If anyone doubted that there was a need for a marine ambulance, they would have had their fears quashed within a week of the Christine's launch. Ronald Tostevin (26) fell some 70ft from cliffs at Portelet, and the Christine was used to assist when it was realised that he could not be rescued from land. The victim had been on a "whoopee float" he hired at Petit Bot, and tried to climb the 100ft high cliffs at Portelet. Although the Christine acquitted itself admirably, the boat had not really been ready for such a mission, lacking the rubber dinghy used to gain easy access to beaches. But a cabin speedboat came to the Christine's aid by following it to the rescue scene and lending the crew a small punt, which was used to pick up Mr Tostevin.

Hundreds of islanders visited St Peter Port Harbour in late June to see the impressive ship The Centurion during its visit to the island. The Centurion was a "mission ship", built by the Society for the Propagation of the Gospel to commemorate its 250th birthday. It was a half-scale replica of the ship that had taken the first Anglican Church missionary to Virginia in 1702. It came to the Channel Islands for a week-long visit, heralded locally by a welcoming party headed by the Bishop of Southampton and watched by hundreds of inquisitive islanders. The visit was uneventful but, shortly after leaving Jersey and Guernsey, The Centurion became involved in a drama at sea. En route to Alderney, the crew saw a pillar of smoke on the horizon to the north. As the smoke grew worse, they realised that it was a ship on fire, so with full sail and engines The Centurion headed for the stricken vessel. On reaching the scene, it found one ship, The Granville, and a great deal of wreckage - a lot of it carrying warnings of explosives. The sunken ship was the Maheage from Antwerp, and after an hour-long search all of the crew were recovered and taken to Cherbourg. The picture, taken by Captain J. Dixon of the Society for the Propagation of the Gospel, shows members of the Centurion crew searching for survivors of the incident, with the Granville in the distance.

1952

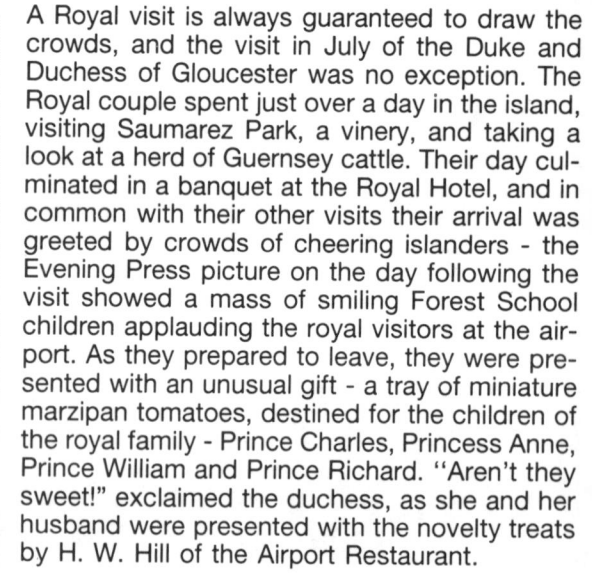

Waterspeed world record holder John Cobb dies in a crash on Loch Ness at 240mph.

A Royal visit is always guaranteed to draw the crowds, and the visit in July of the Duke and Duchess of Gloucester was no exception. The Royal couple spent just over a day in the island, visiting Saumarez Park, a vinery, and taking a look at a herd of Guernsey cattle. Their day culminated in a banquet at the Royal Hotel, and in common with their other visits their arrival was greeted by crowds of cheering islanders - the Evening Press picture on the day following the visit showed a mass of smiling Forest School children applauding the royal visitors at the airport. As they prepared to leave, they were presented with an unusual gift - a tray of miniature marzipan tomatoes, destined for the children of the royal family - Prince Charles, Princess Anne, Prince William and Prince Richard. "Aren't they sweet!" exclaimed the duchess, as she and her husband were presented with the novelty treats by H. W. Hill of the Airport Restaurant.

Hotel guests in their nightwear and the owners of the Palm Court Hotel, Glategny Esplanade (left), were evacuated when the building was badly damaged by fire early in the morning of 2 October. Thousands of pounds worth of damage was estimated to have been done by the blaze, which firemen put out some 45 minutes after arriving at the scene. Neighbouring properties were unaffected. For hotel owners Mr and Mrs Wyndham-Birch it was a personal tragedy. They had been married only since April, and lost all their personal possessions including their wedding presents in the fire. It was thought that the blaze started in the residents' upstairs lounge - the front part of the hotel was completely burned out. But despite the tragedy, and in a show of good old Guernsey pluck, later the same day Mr Wyndham-Birch opened the hotel bar for business as usual.

Roger Bannister runs first four-minute mile. Walt Disney's Peter Pan goes on general release.

1953

35

The first load of anthracite from the grounded cargo ship Fermain is offloaded by lorry on a man-made causeway to the north of St Sampson's Harbour. The Fermain ran aground near the Vale Castle in January while attempting to enter port. The causeway consisted of 3,000 tons of rock and boulders and although it led to the recovery of the ship's cargo nothing could be done to save the ship. Attempts to refloat her failed and she was finally dismantled, bit by bit.

The rebirth of an industry: Ship repairing and surveying returned to the island with the building of the John Upham (Marine) Ltd. slipway at St Sampson's Harbour. The Arrowhead (right) was the first steel ship to enter the new shipyard for repairs.

1953

Royal yacht Britannia is launched. DNA starts to be unravelled. Japan is allowed self-government.

The Forest parish marked the Coronation with a special party and this floral archway surrounded by gaily dressed young people. The Coronation also seemed a good reason to hold a street party. In Route Isabelle 120 boys and girls attended a party where Winkle the clown was the centre of attention. The youngsters also planted four trees to mark the occasion and enjoyed a two-hour bus ride, games and a huge tea.

Muratti day again and another of those biennial Caesarean invasions. Hordes of Jersey fans arrive at the New Jetty on the special excursion steamer Isle of Sark.

Everest is climbed by Edmund Hillary and Sherpa Tenzing Norgay. Queen Elizabeth II crowned. Korean War ends.

1953

The big fish invasion of 1953. Hundreds of islanders and visitors cram the Castle Cornet breakwater during the great mackerel glut of that summer. Thousands of the 'scavengers of the sea' swam close to the shore as islanders recorded record catches. Some of them used just string with pins tied to the end to catch the fish, while it was even suggested some were caught by hand! Meanwhile, millions of whitebait infested the shores. Fishing experts put this sort of invasion down to the presence of porpoises in the area.

Low water on a spring tide was the time for ormer gatherers to head for the beach. The hardy souls who were prepared to wade into the sea were rewarded with catches measured in dozens apiece.

1953

Russian atom spies the Rosenbergs are executed in the US. John F. Kennedy marries Jacqueline Bouvier.

Hollywood film star Olivia de Havilland arrives at Guernsey airport for her first visit to the island where her father, Mr Walter de Havilland, spent his boyhood. Both Miss de Havilland's father and grandfather attended Elizabeth College and the family lived at Havilland Hall. Her grandfather, the Rev. Charles Richard de Havilland, was at one time military chaplain in Guernsey. An Oscar winner, Miss de Havilland starred in many film classics, notably Gone With The Wind.

The day 'The Duke' got married. Guernsey and Spurs' soccer star Len Duquemin ties the knot to his most ardent soccer fan, Tottenham girl June Wakeling, at the Church of St Mary The Virgin, Tottenham. Seven hundred friends and relatives packed the church while extra police had to be drafted in to control the large crowd outside the church. Later that same Saturday Len led out Spurs in front of an even bigger crowd at White Hart Lane. Spurs lost that match 3-2.

The Broad Walk limes at Cambridge Park came in for a severe lopping in the first month of coronation year.

All Comet airliners grounded after mysterious crash off Elba. Marilyn Monroe marries baseball hero Joe DiMaggio.

1954

Smell from the past. In the days when tomato was king, greenhouse soil was sterilised most winters, the damp steam wafting around the neighbourhood with its rich smell. Steaming went on 24 hours a day - there were pipes to move, ground to dig, the boiler to feed with anthracite, and food and drink were needed to help workers cope with the back-breaking task.

1954

US hydrogen bomb destroys Bikini Atoll.
Viet Minh overrun Dien Bien Phu in Vietnam, wiping out the French garrison.

It was an embarrassing accident for the pilot of this Sunderland flying boat when he arrived outside St Peter Port Harbour. He struck a rock on touchdown at North Beach, tearing a hole in the hull. The flying boat settled in the sea and was brought into the harbour where it floated with tail well out of the water but with the cockpit submerged. There was an unauthorised passenger aboard, former Press employee Monica Roger who had cadged a lift back to her home. The Sunderland was later towed to the Careening Hard where for days it was a popular attraction for islanders who clambered through the hull. It was declared incapable of repair and was cut up and removed.

European Convention on Human Rights comes into effect. Algerian War starts.

1954

One of Guernsey's housing estates was beginning to take shape this year and on the front page of the Evening Press was this picture of new flats at Victoria Avenue, St Sampson's.

In September an Aer Lingus Dakota, bound from Dublin via Guernsey to Jersey, missed the runway and landed on a hedge instead. No-one was injured in the incident, but a cow belonging to young farmer Eugene Etasse in a nearby field was killed when it was hit by a propeller.

1954

First nuclear power station opens at Obninsk, USSR. End of post-war rationing in Britain.

Ideal summer weather greeted the Duke and Duchess of Gloucester when they visited the Islands in July for a two-day visit. The royal itinerary included a trip to the annual agricultural show at Saumarez Park. Here they are received by the Bailiff, Sir Ambrose Sherwill, and Lady Sherwill at a glittering reception given by the States at St George's Hall.

Guernsey scored a famous victory in the Muratti this year with young striker Micky Brassell scoring four times in the 5-3 win over Jersey in front of 10,960 people at Springfield. Guernsey captain Alan Hunter holds the vase aloft as he stands on the Jersey quay.

Jamaican immigrants flock to Britain. The Spanish monarchy is reinstated by dictator General Franco.

1955

43

The problem of roadworks in the island is not a new one. The 25 January 1955 Evening Press caption for this photograph reads: 'Love's labour lost – and the taxpayer pays! – Grande Rue, St Martin's, has just been re-laid and re-surfaced in a road-widening project. Yesterday, one of the public services, the Telephone Dept., was tearing up part of the new surface.'

An ambitious sports complex was suggested for the 'unsightly sand pit on the west coast' – the area at Mare de Carteret, between Cobo and Grandes Rocques. The plans included an Olympic-sized swimming pool, changing rooms, tennis courts, a putting green and car parking. The Natural Beauties Committee approved the scheme in principle but the project did not come to fruition.

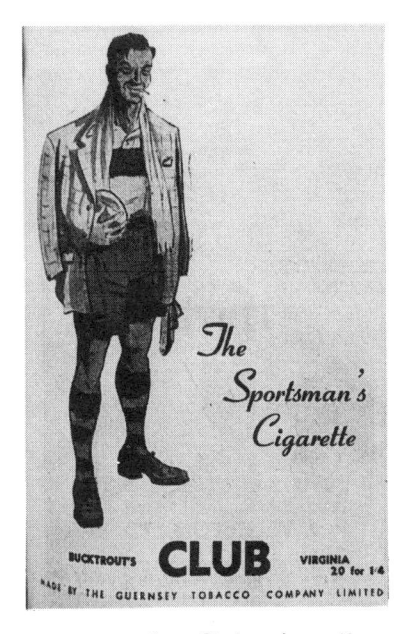

Advertisement for Club cigarettes, produced by local company Bucktrout's, which were hailed as 'The Sportsman's Cigarettes'. A packet of 20 sold for 1s 4d (7p).

44 **1955** Devastating floods leave 400,000 homeless in Australia. Winston Churchill resigns as prime minister of UK.

New equipment installed at the St Martin's and Castel telephone exchanges brought the first ever local dial telephones into use. The island-wide changeover to dial telephones was expected to be complete within eight years and was to mark the beginning of the end for the 'hello girls' who manned the telephone exchanges.

Le Riche's Stores Ltd leads the way in modern store development. The original branch shop at St Sampson's was entirely rebuilt and enlarged to include a modern self-service department. This was 'equipped with the latest hygienic fittings and all provisions will be displayed in modern refrigerated counters.' The building now houses The Press Shop, The Bridge.

First McDonald's hamburger outlet opens in California. Einstein dies. Post-war occupation of Germany ends.

1955

The White Rock, St Peter Port, is a hive of activity as the tomato export season reaches its peak. Two lorries are being unloaded in this picture, while 20 others await their turn.

'Goodbye to Fort Houmet!' The 99-year-old barracks at Fort Houmet, Vazon, are demolished by a party of Royal Engineers. The Lt-Governor, Sir Thomas Elmhirst, fired the first charge. The demolition of the barracks left an earlier tower and battery built of Cobo stone, and a German bunker, as the fort which we know today.

1955

Ruth Ellis hanged at Holloway Prison for murder. Disneyland opens in California. Screen rebel James Dean dies in car crash.

Television viewers in the Channel Islands received their first regular television transmission from Les Platons, Jersey, courtesy of the BBC's 'experimental service'. Electrical shops in St Peter Port were reported to be crowded with hundreds of televiewers, many of whom were seeing television pictures for the first time. 'It is an established fact that television has the power to hold the complete attention of the majority of viewers and, in many cases, is the means of transforming the pattern of home life,' read one article. Another warned of 'the impact of TV on young minds'.

Guernsey's Bill Spurdle becomes the first Channel Islander to take part in an F.A. Cup final. The Manchester City player was reported to have played 'a grand game'.

Hurrah! for **TELEVISION**

Yes — it really is a great occasion for all of us. The family will agree it is the perfect entertainment for a winter's evening at home.

What better time to introduce it to your family circle than NOW !

It's Exciting ! It's Real ! It's Here !

T/V FOR ALL

MURPHY · PYE · PHILIPS · G.E.C.

All Famous Names in Television
IN STOCK AT

Munro's

15, THE POLLET

Est. 1919   'Phone 1071

Racial turmoil splits Alabama, USA. 'Terrorist' Archbishop Makarios deported from Cyprus by British.

1956

Waterskiing in the Old Harbour, St Peter Port, in mid-afternoon sunshine.

Maintenance work on one of the Guernsey Press Co's Cossar printing presses at Le Marchant Street, St Peter Port.

48 **1956** First video tape demonstrated in Chicago. American playwright Arthur Miller marries Marilyn Monroe.

In March police found 38 German detonators and 11 anti-personnel mines within a few feet of cliff paths at Fermain. The pictures show a controlled explosion of one of the detonators. It was found by 14-year-old John Becquet and PC Bichard is seen holding it.

Jehovah's Witnesses held a service at La Vallette bathing pools on 3 June 1956, when eight people were baptised.

RAF planes chase UFOs over Suffolk. Britain's first nuclear station opens at Calder Hall.

1956

49

Swimmers at St Sampson's breakwater prepare for their swim from Guernsey to Herm. All the girls in the top picture completed the swim but only four of the boys were successful.

Herm launch the Martha Gunn, a 45-foot Brighton beach boat, became stuck on a reef 100 yards from Herm Harbour after going on a morning cruise. Skipper Bonny Newton fell overboard and was saved, and 20 frightened holidaymakers were taken off the boat.

1956

Soviet tanks crush Hungarian uprising. Britain and France invade Suez Canal Zone, petrol rationing follows.

This American Dodge caused a great deal of interest when it arrived in Guernsey in May. The car was brought to the island by Mr and Mrs James Griffiths, who came on holiday from Venezuela. They are seen leaving the island on their return trip to England.

The first stork to be seen in the Channel Islands was spotted by two children on top of a tree at Havilland Hall on 16 April. The picture of the three foot long bird, with six foot wing span, long red legs and bill, was taken by Evening Press photographer Ken McLeod.

Guernsey's first pet shop, in St James' Street, St Peter Port, opened in March. Schoolchildren flocked to see one of the first inhabitants of the shop, Lucky the Capuchin monkey, who arrived from a Cheshire Zoo. Pet lovers could order anything from parrots to alligators from the shop.

Britain explodes first hydrogen bomb on Christmas Island. Cavern Club opens in Liverpool.

1957

51

Tragedy struck Sark in October 1957. Stocks Hotel annexe was gutted in a fire on the night of 18 October. A woman who had gone back into the blazing annexe to rescue a dog died of asphyxia. The dog perished, too. Three other dogs and a number of people sleeping in the 10-roomed house escaped from the choking smoke.

PC Peter Castle was a familiar visitor to island schools in the 1950s and 60s lecturing youngsters on road safety. The latest in visual aids, like Noddy and Big Ears puppets, were used to help instill road sense and pupils were shown how to keep their bicycles in tip-top safety shape.

1957

Malaysia gains independence. US soldiers protect young blacks bussing to school at Little Rock, Arkansas.

Malta'd milk. Before dawn on 2 January five Guernsey farmers made their way to the airport with stock destined to be Malta's first Channel Islands' cattle. Six in-calf heifers and a 13-month-old bull were flown to the George Cross island on board a Dakota which refuelled at Nice.

Guernsey footballers hit national headlines long before the days of Matt Le Tissier. Nottingham Forest, Coventry and Manchester City were all glad to make use of local talent in the 1950s. But the local lad made most good was always The Duke, Tottenham Hotspur centre forward Len Duquemin. He became a proud father in March 1957. For the record books Keith Leonard was born to June at the Tottenham home of Duke's mother-in-law. Keith weighed in at 8lb 8oz.

Treaty of Rome signed, allowing formation of EEC. Jerry Lee Lewis records Great Balls of Fire.

1957

More than 6,000 island schoolchildren assembled on Cambridge Park to greet royal visitors The Queen and Prince Philip. A busy Friday 26 July included an assembly of the feudal Chief Pleas at St George's Hall and hearing a loyal address delivered in Latin by Elizabeth College scholar of the year Robert Mahy.

An RAF Valletta aircraft crashed into a bulb field after overshooting the Guernsey Airport runway on 2 November. It gave the eight Elizabeth College cadets and their officer on board a memorable training flight. Fortunately there were no injuries. Unable to land in Guernsey because of the incident, a second Valletta with another group of cadets had to divert to Jersey.

1957

Major radiation leak at Windscale, Cumbria. Jodrell Observatory near Manchester starts stargazing. Russia puts dog Laika into orbit.

A good breeze made the sailing events at the St Peter Port Regatta interesting in August, 1957. Guernsey fishing boats under sail added a picturesque touch while there was sculling in the Old Harbour. The regatta as such is no more though its spirit lives on in the annual Round Table Water Carnival.

The Bailiwick's rarest form of accident, a train crash, occurred in Alderney on 3 December. A truck crashed into the Admiralty stone train at the bottom of Braye Road. Perhaps fortunately, Molly the engine was pushing a train of empty trucks back towards Mannez quarry at the time of the incident.

Daffodils were a familiar sight and a popular export when, in 1957, a mild winter produced an early crop of the 'yellow gold'. By early March 200 boxes of flowers had been exported from Herm.

European Economic Community – France, Italy, West Germany, Belgium, Holland and Luxembourg – comes into being.

1958

55

Tektronix set up their first electronics factory at Victoria Avenue, St Sampson's (above). The firm was to become a major employer in the island over the next three decades.

Amanda water scooters were popular with children and the young at heart (right). Rides around the Model Yacht Pond and sibling races were sought after treats.

1958

First parking meters in London. Manchester United team virtually wiped out in Munich air crash. CND tries to 'Ban the Bomb'.

This Ford Consul crashed 15ft from the Victoria Pier on to the deck of the 30-ton ketch Airy Mouse on a Saturday afternoon in May 1958. Both the boat and the car were badly damaged, but no one was hurt.

Coastal defences at Rocquaine Bay remain an issue occasionally raised today, but in February 1958 something desperately needed to be done. About 80 feet of roadway and footpath subsided following heavy seas, and workmen battled against the clock and the next high tide to carry out repairs.

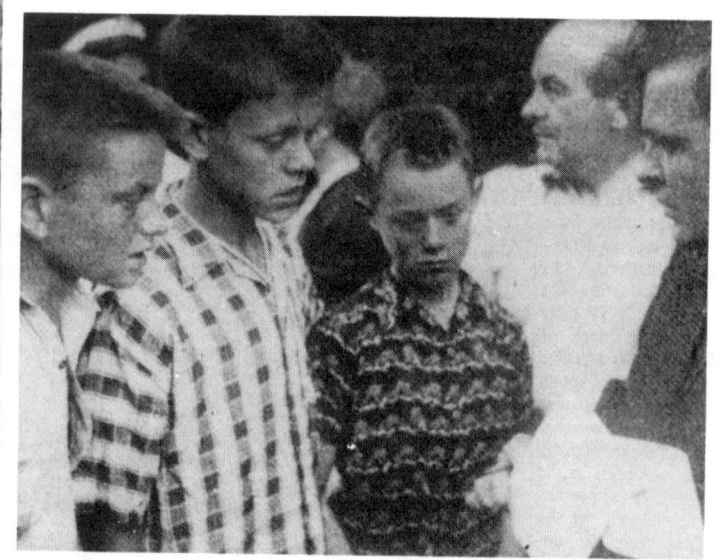

St John Ambulance chief Reg Blanchford saved 14-year-old holidaymaker David Burt (third from left in the photograph) literally by the scruff of his neck on a 200ft cliff near Petit Bot. The boy, who had been clinging on to the near-vertical cliff face for nearly an hour, was only saved when Mr Blanchford grabbed his shirt collar as the rock crumbled away during the rescue. Mr Blanchford said it was a 'miracle' that the boy was still alive.

Kruschev comes to power in Kremlin. Algerians demand independence from France. First yellow lines on some British roads.

1958

A day of bad weather in August 1958 upset nearly 1,000 people's holiday. They were waiting to leave the island by aeroplane but no flights got in or out of the island during the day. Twenty nine stranded holidaymakers ended up spending the night in the Odeon cinema.

A new Lt-Governor was sworn in on 11 December 1958. Vice-Admiral Sir Geoffrey Robson took the oath of office in the Royal Court, watched by jurats, Crown Officers, court officials and the island's rectors.

Motorists on the Forest Road had a shock when this Cambrian Airways Dakota overran the former north-south grass runway, ploughed through a bank and came to rest on the edge of the road. Thirty passengers flying from Jersey to Liverpool were unhurt and the aircraft was undamaged.

1958

Race riots in Notting Hill, London. First trans-Atlantic jet services. US nuclear submarine Nautilus sails under North Pole.

The pilot of this Jersey Airlines four-engined Heron aircraft had a lucky escape when the plane overshot the eastern perimeter of the airport and crashed into a greenhouse. The pilot's cabin was ripped open but he escaped with only slight injuries. The plane, carrying the national newspapers to the island, was trying to land in thick fog.

Ninety one Guernsey cows worth more than £5,000 and another 18 from Sark were sent to Alderney during the year to replenish the island's farms which had been ravaged by foot and mouth disease. The northern isle lost more than 200 cattle and 200 pigs in the outbreak. Islanders, and Evening Press, Star and Jersey Evening Post readers, raised £2,222 in a special appeal to help the farmers.

Jersey potato farmers turned to Guernsey when they suffered acute shortages of workers when it was time to harvest the potato crop in June. A number of islanders went to work in Jersey, where it was reported they could easily earn £12 or £13 a week with overtime.

Fidel Castro comes to power in Cuba. Henry Cooper becomes British and European heavyweight boxing champion.

1959

Bad news heralded the beginning of 1959 when swine fever hit Bob Froome's farm at Le Vallon. This highly infectious pig disease had not been seen in the island for 30 years, but 21 porkers, a pedigree Landrace boar and nine breeding sows had to be destroyed. As the States had no compulsory slaughter policy for swine fever, Mr Froome received no compensation.

Guernsey Young Farmers' entry 'Chinese Dragon' won the Senior Prix d'Honneur at the Battle of Flowers. In spite of a shortage of flowers and fewer entries than normal, some 16,000 paid to see the event on the Thursday.

1959

Russia's Lunik II lands on the Moon. Soon after Lunik III produces the first pictures of the dark side of the Moon.

The first exports from oscilloscope manufacturers Tektronix were said to be imminent. Manager Al Hannmann said that Tektronix and Guernsey would be known in many parts of the world – if all went well. It went well for another 30 years.

Another first in 1959 was the bulk cargo of butane liquid petroleum gas. It was delivered by the MV Kitte Tholstrup to St Sampson's for Kosangas (CI) Ltd. By 1960, it was reported, the Guernsey Gas Light Co. would be taking a supply of commercial butane for the manufacture of an improved, sulphur-free gas for the mains supply.

Flower exports were booming, and the usual shipping arrangements were being supplemented by the first air freight. This Silver City Bristol Freighter was hurriedly chartered to meet demand in late March.

Icelandic gunboats fire on British trawlers in Cod War. First hovercraft launched at Cowes, Isle of Wight.

1959

The changing face of St Peter Port. Demolition work starts at the South Esplanade in preparation for the Albany House development of shops and offices. Two weeks later the States agreed to slash income tax from 5s 2d (26p) to 4s. (20p), the move which was to help Guernsey on the road to economic success.

This Napoleonic tower standing near the top of Victoria Avenue, was demolished to make way for the Housing Authority's Bellegreve Flats.

An appeal was opened to support the on-going costs of the upkeep of the first ever marine ambulance, Flying Christine. After seven years, maintenance costs were mounting and money was needed. A month later the Evening Press reported that the Flying Christine 'may have to be withdrawn' because only £121 had been raised towards the £300 needed for maintenance.

1959

The Dalai Lama flees Tibet and communist Chinese. Postcodes introduced in the UK. Antarctica preserved for scientific research.

The States purchased Fort George for £24,108. 10s 6d, and while it was thought that they had a housing project in view, the Evening Press suggested that an area of some 10 acres should be devoted to 'an island sports centre'. The newspaper said it would reduce delinquency and 'produce a higher standard of wellbeing in the younger generation'. Open market houses were built there instead.

After centuries the ancient feudal custom of Corvee was abolished by Sark's Chief Pleas. The custom was to give the lord of the manor one day's unpaid labour, and applied especially to sea defences and fortification against foreign invaders. Here 11 Sarkees, carrying out their corvee before the law changed, make the cliff near Maseline Harbour safe by bringing down overhanging granite.

Princess Margaret visited the Bailiwick with due pomp and ceremony. After visiting Alderney and Sark, she opened Les Beaucamps School and then attended a ball given by the States at St George's Hall.

Prime Minister Harold Macmillan predicts 'winds of change'. Dead Sea Scrolls found in Israel.

1960

William Arnold was sworn in as Bailiff of Guernsey in the Royal Court on 18 January. The ceremony was unique as it was the first one in the long history of the post to be attended by both the Lt-Governor of Jersey and the First Deemster and Clerk of the Rolls of the Isle of Man.

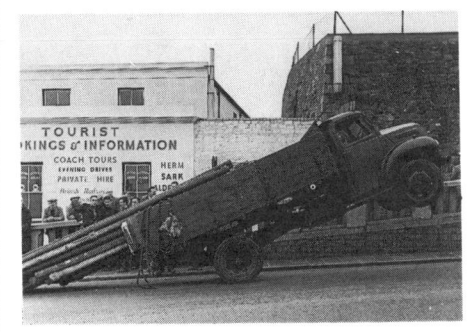

The driver of this C. H. Fuzzey lorry was left with a red face when the load of pipes the vehicle was carrying slid backwards and lifted the cab off the ground just as it passed the Town Church.

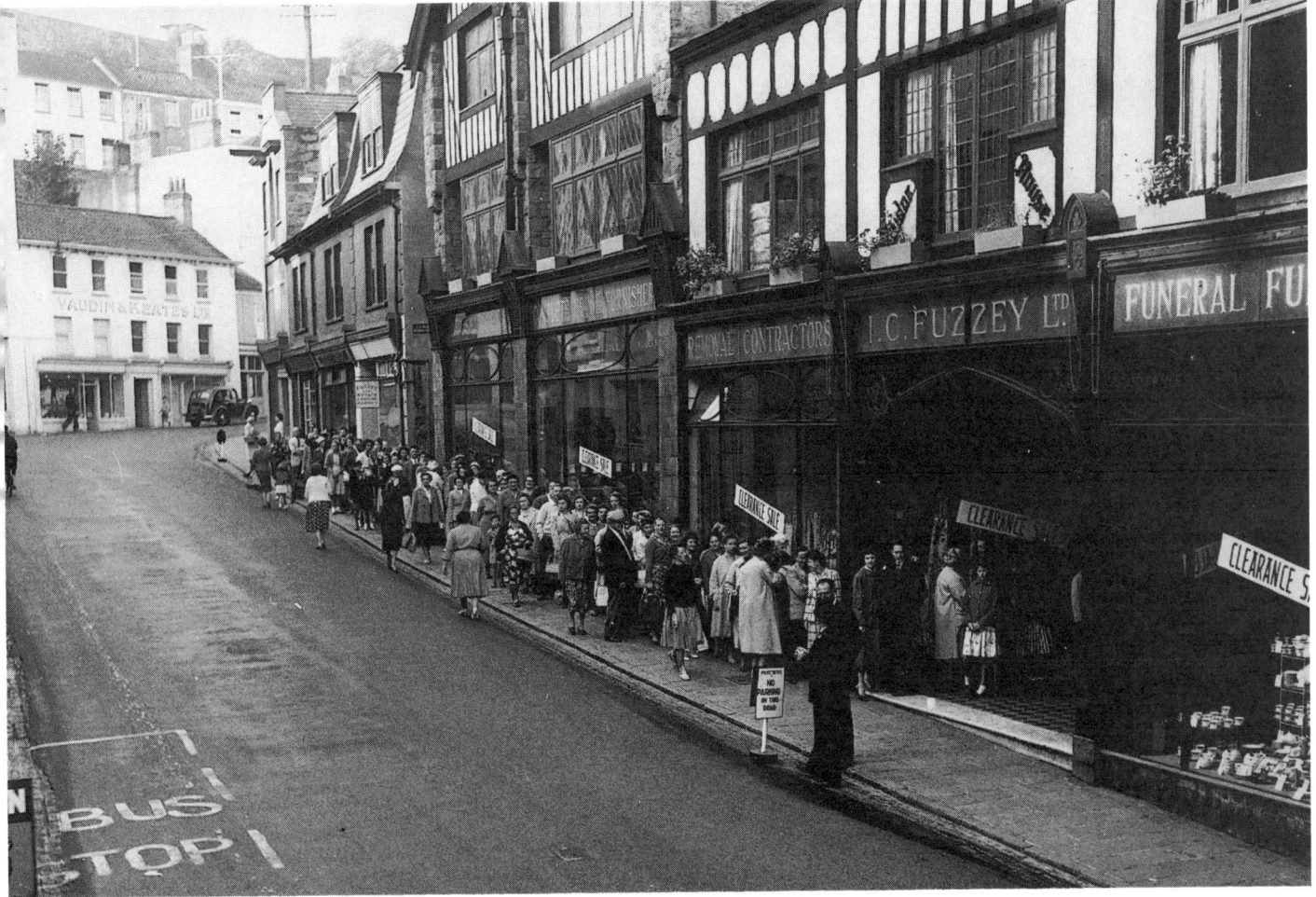

Clearance sale at I. C. Fuzzey's Tudor House store before the site is redeveloped.

1960

Sharpville massacre in South Africa, 56 die.
Death of film star Clark Gable.

The ferry St Julien (left) comes alongside the New Jetty in a stiff easterly breeze.

The new passenger ship Sarnia (above) was named by the wife of the Bailiff in September at the J. Samuel White yard, Cowes, Isle of Wight. The 3,800 ton vessel was a sister ship to the Caesarea which was launched earlier in the year.

An unofficial seamen's strike paralysed shipping movements (left) with some passengers waiting for days to reach the island. Cargo, including fresh meat, had to be flown into the island.

The Herm speedboat Spring Flight I was stolen from its moorings in St Peter Port Harbour in July and found wrecked on the shore of Herm. The Royal Court found the perpetrator guilty of stealing the boat and sentenced him to 18 months in prison. Later in the summer, the Spring Flight III sank at its moorings.

Australian Jack Brabham wins Formula One championship.

1960

Bels' captain Les Collins is held aloft by Reuben Le Poidevin (left) and Peter Powell after his team's 3-1 win over Oaklands in the Upton. Collins, Morris Gallienne and Johnny Queripel scored for the Guernsey champions, while Rex Diamond missed a penalty.

Hans Gies, who was, for three months, commandant of the island during the Occupation, returned to Guernsey during May to celebrate his ruby wedding. He was a major in Infantry Regiment 584 when he held command.

Fire destroyed the machine shop and timber store at the Piette Saw and Planing Mills in September causing £25,000-worth of damage. It took 18 firemen to control the big blaze.

1960

Agadir earthquake kills 12,000 in Morocco.
John F. Kennedy becomes president of the United States.

The Guernsey Rifle Club hold a shoot at the Fort Le Marchant range. The windowless Victorian part of the fort was later demolished because it had become unsafe.

The island moved into the turboprop era of aircraft with both the Dart Herald and Viscount being introduced by British European Airways. The four-engined Viscount was hailed as luxury travel with a 55-minute flight to Gatwick.

The Amalgamated Committee, owners of the Track, gave the go-ahead in March for a kart track to be built around the perimeter of the football pitch at a cost of £1,000. Within a few months the new facility was open and Chick Robilliard won the Channel Islands individual championship on it in September as Guernsey hammered Jersey in the team inter-insular.

Farthing no longer legal tender in UK. US severs diplomatic links with Cuba – Bay of Pigs invasion fiasco.

1961

When it was proposed that developers be allowed to turn Fort George into a housing estate strong feelings were aroused. More than 10,000 islanders signed a petition (above), organised by Michael Marshall, opposing the demolition of the fortress. The issue even featured in Cecil Cook's pantomime at Christmas.

The first yellow and black H plates (above) appeared on hire cars, serving a useful warning that the driver might not be too familiar with local driving conditions.

The first zebra crossing was introduced close to the Royal Hotel in April (left). Other crossings became zebras during the year. It was one of the first signs that traffic was developing into a problem for the island.

1961

Copenhagen's apprentice barbers end their strike – it started in 1938. Berlin Wall goes up.

A Jersey defender clears his lines under pressure from Guernsey's Barry Mahy. A large crowd watched the Muratti final at The Track, which Jersey won 2-1.

North became the first Guernsey team to win the Upton Park trophy in Jersey since the end of the Second World War when they beat Beeches Old Boys 2-0 with goals by Derek Mechem and Barry Mahy. The picture shows supporters at St Helier Harbour.

Israelis snatch Nazi war criminal Adolf Eichmann from Argentina. First major performance by Bob Dylan.

1961

A Silver City Bristol freighter coming in to land from Cherbourg hit a tree and crashed into a field at Les Prevosts, St Saviour's, at the beginning of November. The aircraft broke into two on impact and the pilot and co-pilot were killed. But the seven passengers and a steward who were in the rear of the aircraft escaped without serious injury.

1961

Russian Yuri Gagarin is first man in space. Briton George Blake jailed for 42 years for spying for Russia.

The new British Rail mail steamer Sarnia (above) arrived in St Peter Port on its maiden voyage in June and the Bailiff, William Arnold, was one of the guests who toured the ship.

The Tomato Marketing Board streamlined the export of the Guernsey Tom in June with the introduction of pallets and trays which speeded up the loading and unloading of lorries and boats.

U2 spy plane pilot Gary Powers freed by Russians. James Hanratty sentenced to hang for murder.

1962

71

Almost unrecognisable three decades ago, this stretch of Bulwer Avenue shows the road before alterations were made. In the days before keen awareness of safety factors, motorists drove daily within feet of the storage tanks and were also free to take the South Side road to the breakwater arm. The building on the left has been demolished to make way for more tanks but the cluster in the distance on the right still exists and forms Commodore's headquarters.

1962

150,000 Ban the Bomb campaigners gather in Hyde Park. War criminal Adolf Eichmann hanged in Israel.

Any political correctness was still a long way ahead when the drag hunt met regularly at various local properties. Possibly the most spectacular setting was Havilland Hall which was a perfect foil for the grandeur of the costumed huntsmen. The activity was enthusiastically supported and the fact that the island does not have a fox population meant the drag could be enjoyed without any concern about wild animal welfare. Government House was another starting point. On 29 November there was a joint meet with the Jersey Drag Hunt. It followed a line through Le Vauquiedor, States Dairy, Grove Farm, Rue Poudreuse, Manor area and on to Les Norgiots and Les Blicqs with the 'kill' at Les Caches. An army of spectators followed in cars, including the Lt-Governor and Lady Robson. Police patrolmen kept the traffic under control. It was the first time since 1937 that the Jersey hounds had visited.

The shape of things to come. Traffic lights arrived in Guernsey at the then exhorbitant rate of £1,422 a set. The first ones were installed at the junction of Braye Road and Route Militaire and were reported to be the first of several planned – a somewhat conservative description given their proliferation today.

Cuban missile crisis – world on the brink of nuclear war until Russia backs down. Algerian War ends.

1962

The island was still reeling from one severe gale when another struck in April. Its dramatic effect left Cobo without a coast road where coastal properties appeared to have a miraculous escape. The westerly gale coincided with very high tides and left a trail of damage and flooding on 5 April. A brief lull allowed some emergency rebuilding but that evening 'the angry sea once again took its toll'. Cobo was worst hit and pounding seas near the Rockmount Hotel breached the wall for 100 feet. It tore away almost the entire width of the road. The sea surged through the gap and flooded Les Pieux Hotel, forcing householders to flee. Work went on all day to fill the cavity but that evening the breach widened and more of the road caved in. Flooding, damage and devastation to growing crops was reported along the entire west coast: 'In all it was a day of heartbreak to the westerners who were still recovering from the battering inflicted by the January storm.'

A severe gale wreaked havoc in Alderney at the end of January. Even 'the tremendous strength' of Alderney breakwater was 'unavailing in the face of the ferocious onslaught'. The breakwater suffered a breach of 120 feet during a 25-minute storm on January 11. The next day the British Railways' Southampton to Jersey ferry had its entrance door torn off by a huge wave and companionways were flooded. The storm also claimed most of the ancient Fort Hommeaux Florains in Alderney after enormous seas broke over it.

1962

Hong Kong puts up wall to keep out Chinese.
Marilyn Monroe found dead from overdose.
Nelson Mandela goes on trial.

A white mantle of snow covered the island in early March. Islanders were forced to retrieve shovels from garden sheds. Grit, or even cinders, was strewn around to try to ease the icy chaos but in the days before four-wheel drive it was a long, slow process getting anywhere. The plus side was time off for schoolchildren and the rare chance to enjoy enough snow for toboganning and snowball fights. The snow arrived on February 27, transforming hamlets like Le Variouf into festive scenes.

While seven-day opening is being pursued today, there was a proposal for Saturday to be considered as a closed day in 1962. The Chamber of Commerce decided that the market should follow banks and close on that day and shops should also shut their doors. The unusual theory was based on a problem with getting supplies to town. Most shops had deliveries only three days a week! Chamber member Mr J. R. Snell admitted that his idea was revolutionary but it gained widespread support among other traders.

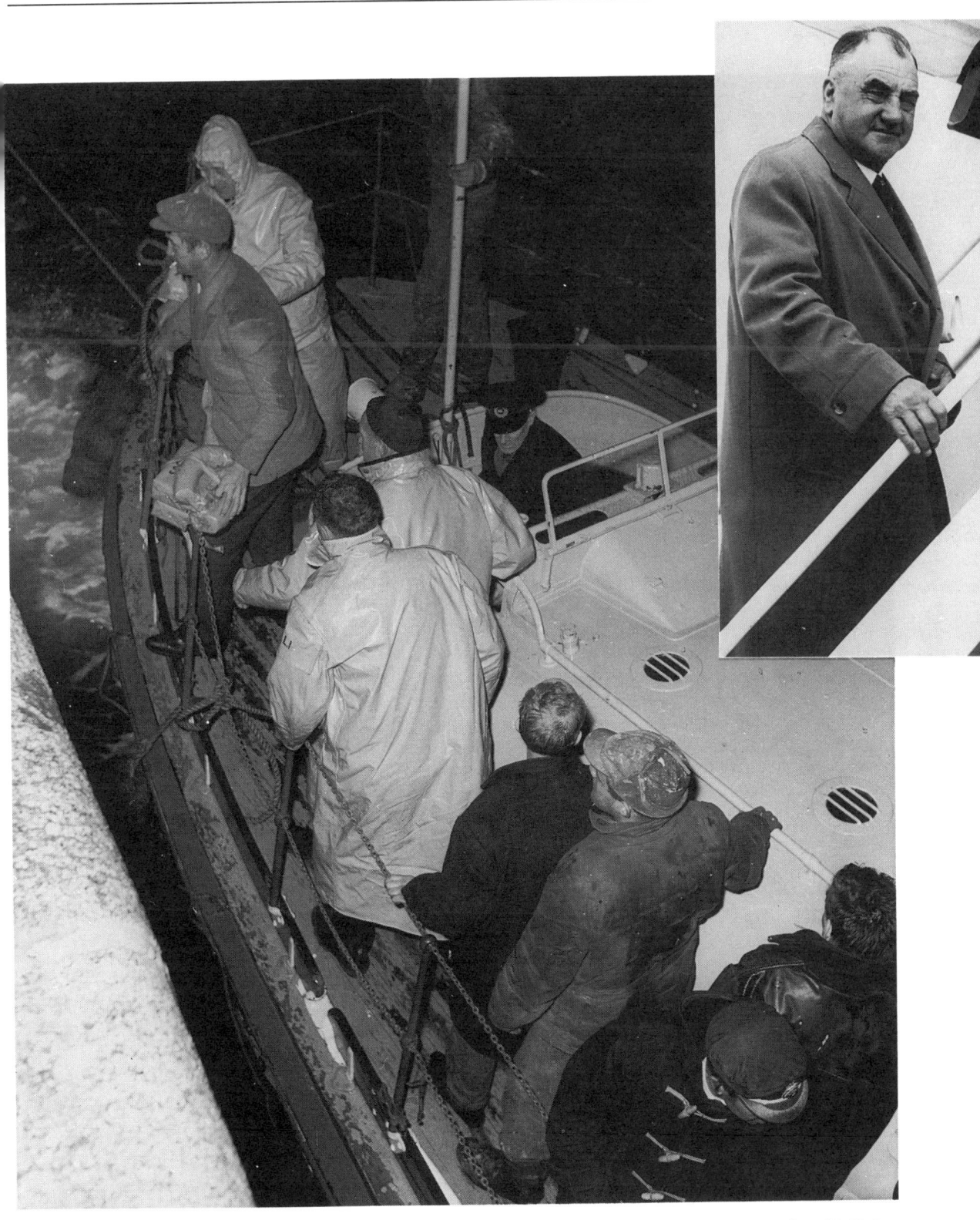

The Pill goes on sale in Britain. France's President De Gaulle says 'Non' to Britain joining EEC. Britain launches first satellite.

1963

After a 15-hour battle with mountainous seas the lifeboat Euphrosyne Kendal returned to St Peter Port with the captain and eight crew of the Norwegian freighter Johan Collett at 6.45am on 6 February. The cargo of zinc ore shifted when the freighter was in heavy seas some 13 miles off Les Hanois and the ship listed some 40 degrees. Water flooded the engine room and stopped the generators in minutes. Captain Leif Moen ordered 13 men into a lifeboat and they were soon picked up by the passing ship Bonnard. Three more crew were picked up by a small boat from the Norwegian tanker Kaupanger. The Euphrosyne Kendal drew alongside at 6.30pm. At one stage the South African warship President Kruger was going to try to tow the casualty, then decided to await a tug from Cherbourg. The tug established the tow just after midnight, but in the terrible conditions the Johan Collett's list worsened. Coxswain Bert Petit (top) brought the lifeboat alongside the freighter and the remaining crew were taken on board and brought to Guernsey. The tug later abandoned the tow and the Johan Collett sank west of Guernsey a couple of hours later. The seamen were later taken to Moore's Hotel, then were flown back to Norway via Jersey the next day. For his part in the rescue Coxswain Petit was awarded the RNLI Gold Medal.

1963

US, Russia and Britain sign nuclear test ban treaty. Island formed by volcano off Iceland. Hot Line links Moscow to Washington.

A January gale tore the marine ambulance Flying Christine from its moorings and pounded it against the harbour wall beneath the Connaught Restaurant. The boat was severely damaged before it was towed into the calm of the Old Harbour, but was found to be beyond repair. Estimates for a replacement were put at £10,000 and an appeal was launched to raise the money. It was soon forthcoming with £500 promised by Sark, and the new vessel, Flying Christine II, was built at C. P. Wilson's Marinecraft premises at Castle Emplacement.

The Bristol Freighter City of London crashed on takeoff, coming to rest in fields just past the western end of the runway. All four people aboard escaped serious injury, but the aircraft was a write-off.

'Third Man' spy Kim Philby escapes to Moscow. Russian Valentina Tereshkova is the first woman in space.

1963

Huge crowds greeted the Queen Mother wherever she went during her visit. She laid the foundation stone for the new Ladies' College building, visited Alderney and Sark and was the guest of honour at Elizabeth College's quatercentenary.

78   **1963**   War minister John Profumo quits amid scandal. Great Train Robbers steal £2.5m. President Kennedy assassinated at Dallas.

The Beatles played to packed houses at Candie auditorium.

Heavy snow fell at the beginning of the year, creating a fairytale land of whitened trees and shrubs.

Beatles enter charts with I Wanna Hold Your Hand. Cassius Clay becomes world heavyweight boxing champion.

1964

Islanders had their first glimpse of the revolutionary hydrofoil Condor 1 in April, 1964, as she was towed into St Peter Port Harbour. The huge cargo liner Neidenfels brought the hydrofoil from Messina in Sicily where it was built. The first Condor cost £200,000 and operated at a cruising speed of 40 mph. She was 91.6ft long and could seat 140. Services between the Channel Islands and St Malo began in May.

1964

Great Train Robbers jailed for total of 307 years. Rolling Stones release first LP. Nelson Mandela jailed for life.

Lt-Governor Sir Charles Coleman is shown the production of Tetrapak milk cartons at the States Dairy.

Grower Ken Le Prevost with a fine crop of chrysanthemums in his nursery at Newhaven, Frie Baton, St Saviour's. He produced one of his best crops ever in this year.

President Johnson signs US Civil Rights Bill prohibiting racial discrimination.

1964

81

An estimated 12,000 islanders and holidaymakers flocked to L'Ancresse (above) for this Guernsey Riding and Hunt Club organised Point to Point Steeplechase meeting.

The day the Stones rolled in with their early trademark scowls and pouts (right). 1,000 beat fans packed into the New Theatre Ballroom to see the Rolling Stones. It was still early days in the Stones' career and with a small repertoire of songs they performed for just half an hour.

Christmas 1964 at Beau Sejour (left) and not a leisure centre in sight, only Father Christmas, two reindeer and a whole lot of local children excited at the prospect of meeting the maker of their dreams.

1964

Britain bans death penalty. Chinese test atom bomb. Great Train Robber Charlie Wilson escapes.

A large crowd turned out to see the launch of the replacement marine ambulance Flying Christine II on 6 July. The ribbon was cut by Lady Coleman, wife of the Lt-Governor.

Tense time for boatmen and Trinity House staff as the Hanois Lighthouse is resupplied and the keepers changed. The moderate swell meant skilled boat handling was needed.

Start of ground war in Vietnam as US sends in 50,000 troops. Rhodesia declares independence.

1965

83

In May the 4,560-ton Liberian freighter La Salle went aground on Le Boin reef, two miles off the west coast between Lihou and Perelle. All 39 crew, including 29 Chinese, were saved by the lifeboat. La Salle later broke her back and sank. The ship had come from Australia with a cargo of oats and was bound for Hamburg.

84   1965   Violent race riots in Watts area of Los Angeles, National Guard called in.
Sir Winston Churchill dies.

About 500ft of Rocquaine coast road or La Route de La Lague collapsed at the end of January after severe battering from heavy seas. Fleets of lorries immediately rushed to dump boulders into the breach to prevent the soft clay behind being further eroded. The repair work lasted months.

Beaucette Quarry was approved in principle as a yacht marina by the States in February, but it was several years before it was completed.

Footballer Stanley Matthews is knighted.
Malcolm X gunned down in New York.

1965

Guernsey's footballers sank to new lows this year, losing their eighth successive Muratti to 'lucky' Jersey 2-4 at the Track on 7 May. Despite this spectacular attempt on goal by Colin Renouf, one of the island's favourite footballing sons and now a successful manager, Jersey were 'let off the hook' after trailing 1-2 and scored twice in the last 10 minutes to win. Rex Bennet summed it up: 'Never will a Jersey goalkeeper play as Peter Osment did. He had some saves that bordered on the incredible.' John Loveridge and Tony Williams scored for the home side.

Five Guernsey people were among 26 people killed when a British United Channel Islands Airways flight crashed on its approach to Jersey airport in thick fog. The five were Town Lloyds Bank manager Mr S. A. Schofield and his wife and two sons aged 12 and 14, and the pilot, 32-year-old Peter Self. The only survivor was 20-year-old French air hostess Dominique Sillere. 'I can't understand why I'm alive, because other passengers were sitting right next to me,' she said.

1965 saw a historic victory for Guernsey over the crapauds in the Siam Cup, a feat rarely matched in many encounters on the rugby pitch. The final score was 6-3 at Les Vauxbelets from three penalties. The winning kick was only adjudged a score by one judge and it was up to the referee to rule for the jubilant home side.

1965

BEA Comet airliner makes first automatic landing. Beatles awarded MBEs, play New York's Shea Stadium.

The 'majestic' block of flats at Cour du Parc was opened on Thursday 22 July by the then Bailiff, Sir William Arnold. He described the £140,000 block, which took more than two years to build, as 'magnificent'. The development was profiled in the Evening Press inside pages under the headlines: New flat tenants will have fine view, and: Spacious rooms in skyscraper.

Island businessmen were fearing the worst in the summer as rumours flew that 300 'beatniks' were to invade the island. A sign was pinned to the door of Maison Carre to deter the 'undesirable visitors'. According to an Evening Press reporter, 'normal customers' objected to the strangely dressed young people. 'Who wants to eat by people with their shoes off?' she asked.

One of the first open market house at Fort George was completed and offered for sale this year (left).

John Lennon says Beatles 'more popular than Jesus'. Kray twins jailed for murder. England wins World Cup.

1966

The 900th anniversary of the island's association with the Crown of England was celebrated by resurrecting the traditional procession – La Chevauchee de St Michel – which, starting in the Vale, wound its way around most of the island. It is thought the Chevauchee procession may have started out as a fertility rite, dating from centuries before the days of feudalism. Traditionally held every three years, the ceremony was given up in 1837. It included a mounted procession of island officials and there was dancing and refreshment at various stops along the route, including La Table des Pions at Pleinmont, Torteval (below, right). Film star Olivia de Havilland, whose father and grandfather were Guernsey-born, visited the island for the 1966 celebrations and presented the prizes for the best old Guernsey costumes. The photograph (above) shows the 'vavasseurs, king's officers and dragoons' taking part in the traditional Dance of Derision round the Druid's altar at Jerbourg, St Martin's.

88   1966   Mao launches Cultural Revolution in China. Aberfan coal tip slide kills 116 Welsh children in their school.

Surfing, described as 'the spectacular and exacting "in" sport of the year'. The first Guernsey Surfboard Club championship, sponsored by Player's Gold Leaf, was held at Vazon Bay. Twenty members of the 35-strong Guernsey club contested the trophy, with seven entries from Jersey in the open event. Among the visitors were four Australians and a Hawaiian, but Guernsey champion Bob Warry came out on top as overall winner of the event.

St George's Hall's long life as a centre of entertainment comes to an end. In its time it housed many trades exhibitions, agricultural and flower shows. It was a conference hall, a roller skating rink and venue for boxing and wrestling matches. In its last days, it proved a popular centre for the youth of the island. More than 900 fans (above) attended a final gig to mark the end of the ballroom's long life. Among the groups that played were My Generation, Humble Fred, and The Other.

Cavern Club in Liverpool goes into liquidation. First meeting in 400 years of heads of Catholic and Anglican churches.

1966

The Tudor House complex at the Bordage, St Peter Port, takes shape. The photograph shows Mill Street and Burnt Lane in the background.

Snow carpets The Bridge, blanking out windows of the cars on the roads in the mid-60s: Ford Anglia estate, Hillman Imp, Morris Minor, Triumph Herald, Riley 1.5, Bedford van, Austin Mini. And there was room to park!

1966

Indira Gandhi is India's first woman prime minister. Moors murderers Ian Brady and Myra Hindley jailed for life for child killings.

Guernsey's new 10-pin bowling centre opens at Lynwood Bowl at First Tower Lane, St Peter Port. The photograph shows a member of staff trying a shot on one of the centre's 12 lanes. Clare Williams, one of Britain's top woman players of the day, was in the island for the opening, and provided instruction for any willing amateurs during the first week.

Sound of Music fever hits Guernsey (left). While cinema-goers queued to see the film at the Gaumont, advertisers took advantage of its popularity to sell anything from cigarettes to vacuum cleaners. 'If you're 16 going on 17, or 18-19 or 20, La Jeunesse has the right clothes for every young lady,' claimed one advertisement. 'Travel to "The Sound of Music" the comfy way in a Cumficab,' suggested another.

The Evening Press' regular feature On The Teen Beat – by Dave Harris kept local youths up to date with the latest trends in fashion and pop music, both in Guernsey and the UK. This bell-bottom trouser suit (right) was modelled at a fashion show at the Cellar Club in St Peter Port. The show was organised by Annette Weysom, proprietor of She Boutique, which sold 'with it' clothes from London.

Castle Cornet is lit up at night. The Evening Press comment said that, although work on the floodlighting was not yet complete, the 'general effect should be very pleasing'.

Six Day War pits Israel against Syria, Jordan and Egypt – Israel wins and doubles in size. Abortion legal in UK.

1967

Shortly before midnight on 13 July the 7,687 ton cargo vessel President Garcia ran aground at Saints Bay. It steamed in at 12 knots, ploughing through fishermen's boats but narrowly missing an anchored yacht with two visitors on board. The ship was carrying copra and was on its way to Rotterdam from the Phillipines when it steamed into the bay to the surprise of two GPO engineers and a courting couple. Two Dutch tugs failed to pull the freighter from the rocks two days later. In the end some of its cargo was taken off to make it lighter and it was pulled off a week later, but not before it drew hundreds of visitors to the area to see it.

The British tanker Constantia S. broke in two when it struck Les Casquets rocks at 11am on Monday 23 January. The 30 crew and ship's dog took to the lifeboats but Captain A. Vlasto stayed on the doomed ship and was later rescued by a French helicopter. The Constantia hit the Point Colotte rock. Half the ship sank and the other half drifted away. The tanker was on its way from Amsterdam to Gibraltar and luckily was not carrying any oil. Most of the crew, pictured here, were picked up by the four man crew on the Trinity House lighthouse tender Burhou. The four men – pilots Nick Allen, J. Quinain, J. Allen and A. Johns – received awards from the Royal National Lifeboat Institution for undertaking the rescue of 20 men from one of the lifeboats.

1967

Biafran war of secession starts in Nigeria. Pirate radio ships outlawed. First motorist breathalysed, in Somerset.

In 1967 Guernsey was exporting ormers to Paris, Dinard, Boulogne and St Brieuc, and even a few to England. While scenes such as this with ormers being weighed and packed for export are unknown now the headline 'Poor Week-end For Ormers' is not! But ormers were beginning to become a luxury item selling at 3s 4d a pound in the market later that year.

In June hotelier Charles Rogers, of St Anthony's, Braye Road, Vale, felt he was being persecuted by the States Water Board who were threatening to cut off his supply so he resorted to the islanders' traditional cry for help and raised the Clameur de Haro. To claim the ancient redress he knelt, invoked the help of Rollo and recited the Lord's Prayer, watched by his wife. He claimed the water meter was faulty and refused to pay the bills.

It was nearly a white Christmas this year with a snow storm on 9 December. Although it gave a festive but icy touch to the island it caused chaos on the roads and grumbles from St Peter Port traders as people chose to stay at home.

'Flower Power' anthem San Francisco enters US charts. Francis Chichester sails around the world single-handed.

1967

The Court of the Fief Anneville met for the first time since 1952 on 18 October (above) and for the first time since 1882 was attended by the Seigneur, Professor Cyril Northcote Parkinson. It was held outside the porch of the ancient Anneville house, near the Camp du Roi, with the purpose of reconstituting the court.

The Muratti final – which fell on Liberation Day – was a sad day for the green and whites who lost 3-1 to Jersey, after extra time, at the Track.

1967

Apollo I astronauts die in launch pad fire. Elvis Presley marries Priscilla. Revolutionary Che Guevara shot dead in Bolivia.

A tide of black oil from the Torrey Canyon threatened to engulf the Bailiwick at the end of March after the tanker ran aground off Cornwall and broke up (below). Gallons of detergent were sprayed on the encroaching oil slick by Royal Navy minesweepers; booms were put across St Peter Port and Braye harbours, and Sark Chief Pleas voted £1,000 to deal with the emergency, but attempts to break it up failed and gallons of black sludge were washed up on west coast beaches. Weeks were spent clearing the beaches (left) and dumping the oil in disused quarries.

A warship at Ladies' Bay made an unusual sight on the morning of 23 August (left). The tank landing craft was carrying two 27-ton armoured bulldozers, two seven and a half ton bulldozers and two dumper trucks, which the Royal Engineers were to use to clear 1,500 tons of rock from Chouet to reach a cache of German ammunition.

US civil rights leader Dr Martin Luther King shot dead. An American buys London Bridge for £1m. and takes it to Arizona.

1968

Summer cabaret was at its height in the mid to late 1960s. This local group (above) is the Black Bottoms, similar to the Black and White Minstrels, who performed at the Wayside Cheer and Royal Hotel. They were very popular with visitors and locals alike. During the day they were teachers, secretaries and professional people. In the picture are Barbara Gradwell, Molly Thompson, Marilyn Roberts, Vicki Small, Chris Davies, Hazel Rowe, Roy Helyar, Richard Hayden, Paul Gradwell, Peter Carre, John Le Huray and Bob Thompson.

Vietnam and the war was much on people's minds during the late 1960s. Elizabeth College students (right) raised a large amount of cash for refugees. One of their stunts was the arrest and subsequent pillorying of a felon in St Peter Port. Simon Chandler was the victim and his captors were Peter Villalard and Pierre Coutanche, all 17.

1968

Legoland Family Park opens at Billund, Denmark. Students riot in Paris. Pope condemns birth control.

Among the island's visitors during 1968 were a group of people from the Welsh village of Aberfan whose village school had been overwhelmed by a slippage in a coal spoil heap with the loss of many young lives. Two groups of 50 and a further 60 were brought to Guernsey for a spring holiday by the Red Cross.

This huge German bunker went on the offensive when the Vardes Quarry rockface above which it stood crumbled away. The huge lump of reinforced concrete tumbled down and crushed a large crawler crane, pushing it deep into mud on the quarry floor.

Wimbledon admits professional players. 300 villagers die in My Lai massacre in Vietnam. Last voyage of the liner Queen Elizabeth.

1968

97

Royal Engineers troops were back in the island in July to assist with the development of Beaucette quarry as a marina. They were to blow a channel between the quarry and the sea but the task proved tougher than expected and they had to return the following year to complete it. The soldiers were unloading stores from the landing ship logistic Sir Percival.

Sister Elizabeth Lincoln was awarded the MBE for her work for Imperial Cancer Research in the 1968 Birthday Honours List. She was pictured with the Lt-Governor, Sir Charles Coleman, at a Government House reception to mark the occasion of The Queen's official birthday.

The Housewives' League was a short-lived 1960s group which attempted to hold back the onset of high prices. Anne Fallaize was one of the leaders. She is seen here on the left during a league march on the market.

1968

Prague uprising crushed by Warsaw Pact tanks. Motor racing ace Jim Clark dies in crash at Hockenheim.

A huge hole appeared in the garden of Edward Solway's home at Rockmount, Delancey. It was believed to have been caused by the collapse of a German tunnel. The 20ft deep cavern was filled in by workers from the States Works Department.

The technological sensation of the late 1960s was the development of the hovercraft. Guernsey was not to be left out and soon a diminutive version was to be seen buzzing around the beach at L'Ancresse. In the driving seat is the builder, Mr C. Rowswell, of Celrose, Coutanchez.

Tomato growing was still a major island industry in 1968. These young plants seen on Mr D. H. Falla's North Brook property are waiting to be sent out to greenhouses all over the island.

One of the island's more distinguished, if incognito, guests during 1968 was the former King Umberto of Italy, pictured leaving the airport with his aide, Sgr Le Conte Pinanzola.

Surf's up. Richard Gillingham and friend ride the waves at Vazon.

American Neil Armstrong is first man on the Moon. Grandmother Golda Meir becomes Israel's prime minister.

1969

Work gets under way on the Grand Bouet housing development where Courtil Ash, Rue des Pins, etcetera, now stand. The crash housing programme was advocated by the States Housing Investigation Committee under Deputy Henry Henchman. It attracted more than its fair share of controversy. Deputy Tom Ogier opposed the compulsory purchase the development required and there was dismay in many quarters that the States went for a non-conventional form of construction and for a developer whose design did not meet the tender specifications. The Bouet development would have been more varied with more open green spaces if it had gone to another builder, but Maxim Construction's tender, £870,000, was the only one of less than £1 million.

A new concrete apron and repairs to the existing sea wall near Le Catioroc aimed at securing the coastline from the sea's battering. In the background are Lihou (left) and the islet Chapelle Dom Hue.

1969

John Lennon marries Yoko Ono. Senator Edward Kennedy escapes from crash at Chappaquiddick Island bridge.

An island that had seen thousands of quarrymen over the years had miners working under it in 1969, and under the waters of Belle Greve Bay, too, where Operation Outfall was under way. When Evening Press reporter Herbert Winterflood went underground in early April the tunnel already ran 800ft beyond the Red Lion sea wall.

A stunned July meeting of Chief Pleas heard the Dame of Sark announce that she was handing the running of Sark over to Guernsey. Dame Sybil Hathaway said the island's government needed reform and criticised members who broke the very laws they made. How, she asked, could the island be promoted as a haven of peace with 42 tractors, few of which observed the traffic laws? La Dame was also tired of having to call in the Guernsey police every few weeks because of 'complaints and the utter disregard for the licensing laws'. But Sark's feudal uniqueness continued under the Seigneurship of La Dame's grandson, Michael Beaumont.

Guernsey got into the world record books in 1969 courtesy of game fisherman Des Bougourd who landed a 430lb porbeagle shark 300 yards off the Minquiers' Pipette Rocks. The monster brought Mr Bougourd to his knees at the end of the fight but record regulations prevented others on board Graham Cowley's trawler, Storm Drift, lending a hand until it came to the gaffing.

First human eggs fertilised in test tube.
Yasser Arafat becomes leader of the PLO.
First flight of Concorde.

1969

On 1 October 1969 the GPO left and its pillar box red vans and boxes took on the Oxford blue hue of the Guernsey Post Office. The new postal administration came under fire from owners and tenants of minor islands who were prohibited from issuing their own carriage label stamps as they had in the past. Brecqhou millionaire Len Matchan (left) operated a one-day helicopter pirate mail service on 30 September. Demand for the 'first and last day' cover was said to be good and the president of the 'Big Brother' Guernsey Post Office Board, Conseiller Peppino Santangelo, was said to have been mailed one by the larger than life businessman 'with my compliments'.

The island was still quite naive about drugs when, in 1969, green-fingered Fred Kreckeler grew a giant mystery plant in the garden of his Rougeval home. Within three months the plant, from a discarded birdseed, had rocketed to 12ft. Gardeners were baffled and the plant remained unidentified – until shortly after a picture was published. The cannabis plant was promptly cut down, folded into the boot of a detective's Triumph Herald, taken away and incinerated.

There were lucky escapes for the Blondin operator at Manuelle's Longue Hougue Quarry and the sexton of St Sampson's Church on Friday 29 August when a huge landslip sent dozens of graves plunging to the quarry floor (right). It also carried away the Blondin overhead bucket's engine house. The 'driver' leapt for his life when he saw the fissures opening. The incident marked the end of quarrying at Longue Hougue which is now a major reservoir.

1969

Paul McCartney marries Linda Eastman.
Voting age lowered from 21 to 18 in Britain.

Beaucette Yacht Marina was taking shape throughout 1969. Questions were asked of the UK Government about the involvement of UK soldiers in a commercial venture. It was said to be a valuable training exercise. The Sappers' involvement in breaking through from the disused quarry to the sea helped keep the cost of the initial development below six figures. In 1995 the marina, now complete with facilities including a leased-out restaurant, was on the market for £1.75 million.

A number of now familiar aspects of island life made their first appearance in 1969. The first filter-in-turn system, an import from Jersey, came into operation at the South Esplanade; Guernsey's first decimal coinage was issued; the Westminster Bank installed the island's first cash machine and, for the first time, the island had a Deputy Bailiff. Mr John Loveridge took his seat in the Royal Court after being sworn in on 23 September.

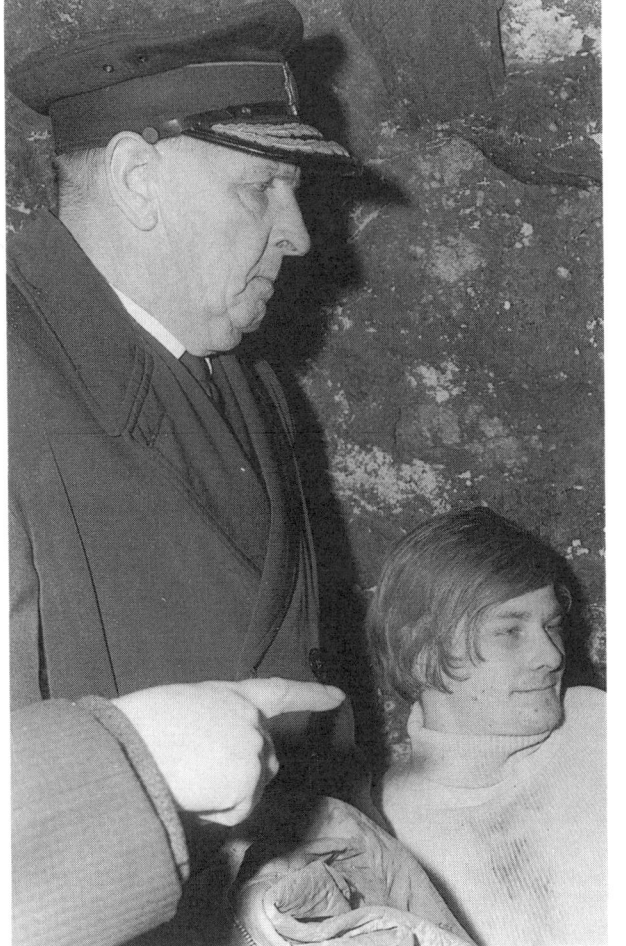

Vietnam war protesters killed at Kent State University. Golfer Tony Jacklin wins US Open.

1970

Guernsey teenagers (above), frustrated at the lack of a decent dance hall in the Town area, decided to take to the streets of St Peter Port to make their voices heard in March. It was a protest that nearly failed to get off the ground, when the three young shop assistants organising the march apparently lost their nerve at the last minute. However, Deputy Edmund Burbridge, vice president of the Sports Committee, was waiting for them at the States offices, and when the three found this out from a Press reporter sent to cover the march, they quickly rustled up some 50 supporters. Following the march, the three leaders spoke to Deputy Burbridge for about half an hour, but were warned not to expect miracles. The three expressed their annoyance that no States money had been allocated for the youth of the island, and said they wanted to see a dance hall 'no smaller than St George's'.

A search for relics of the German occupation nearly ended in tragedy for four youths, when one of them collapsed in the entrance shaft of a network of tunnels beneath the hillside at La Valette. The youth, 18-year-old Roy Fallaize, had been unable to squeeze himself through a foot wide gap into the open air. It took two firemen 30 minutes to get him to the surface, and he was taken to hospital suffering from exposure and stomach pains. Roy and three friends (Marcel Rogers, Michael Le Flem and Bimbo Dodd) had discovered a small cave which led to the tiny gap in the tunnel. At the back of this three foot deep cave was a 12ft drop to the tunnel floor. Equipping themselves with torches and rope, they set out to look for relics. After exploring for a while, they noticed a strange smell and, thinking it could be poisonous, they went to leave. It was as they were leaving that Roy fainted. His friends tried to rescue him but were unable to get him out of the shaft. The Fire Brigade were eventually called by Detective Constable John Barlow, who happened to be passing, and Roy was rescued. The picture shows fire chief Frank Murrell, who led the rescue operation, and Marcel Rogers. Minutes after the rescue the Public Works Department sent men to fill the cave with rocks, and later tons of concrete were poured into the shaft to seal it.

1970

Biafran civil war reaches bitter end, famine looms. First Boeing 747 jumbo jet crosses Atlantic. Pink Floyd headline at Hyde Park.

Was he mad, after publicity, or just another bold soul looking for adventure? When local crooner Noel de Carteret (left) announced that he intended to sail non-stop to Norway in an 11ft 6in. rubber sailing dinghy, the experts had no doubt into which category he fell. But despite their suggestion that he might be better off behind a microphone, Mr de Carteret was determined, and after announcing his plans he set out on the 1,000 mile journey secretly at dusk on the morning of 25 September. The 39-year-old had no food with him and planned to exist solely on a diet of raw fish, plankton and sea water. He had only fishing tackle, a transistor radio (receiver only) and faith in the theories of French scientist Alain Bombard, who had taken the journey previously. Poor weather in the English Channel at that time of year was one reason why he was advised against the trip, and it was bad weather that put paid to his ambitions some three days later, when a gale forced him to put into Exmouth. The attempt was abandoned, although Mr de Carteret said he intended to try again.

Guernsey's acute housing shortage was alleviated somewhat when new homes at the Bouet in St Peter Port were opened in November, with one resident declaring of her Courtil Ash flat: "It's smashing!" Fine weather during the summer helped the project move ahead.

First all-metal liner, Brunel's ss Great Britain, brought back to Bristol from the Falklands.

1970

An £824,000 plan to bring the cargo handling facilities at the White Rock up to date and to make essential repairs got under way in March, when plant to be used in the work arrived. The work involved clearing the existing buildings on berths four and five, providing a "false quay" in front of number four berth, buying two 32-ton capacity cranes and creating a new deep water berth by removing rock from number four berth. The plan was to create an area that would meet the growing demand for container handling facilities. Pictures show plant arriving at the harbour, and the start of demolition work on number four berth.

1970

Rock singer Janis Joplin dies of heroin overdose. Alexander Solzhenitsyn wins Nobel Prize for literature.

What was described at the time as "the largest single project ever undertaken by the States" came to fruition in May when the power station was opened at North Side, Vale. It was opened by the Lt-Governor, Vice-Admiral Sir Charles Mills (right), and heralded as one of the most advanced stations of its type in the world. The Evening Press reported that it was "viewed with respect by engineers, journalists and others at the opening ceremony". Sir Charles was shown around the station by engineer manager Ian Young after the official opening ceremony.

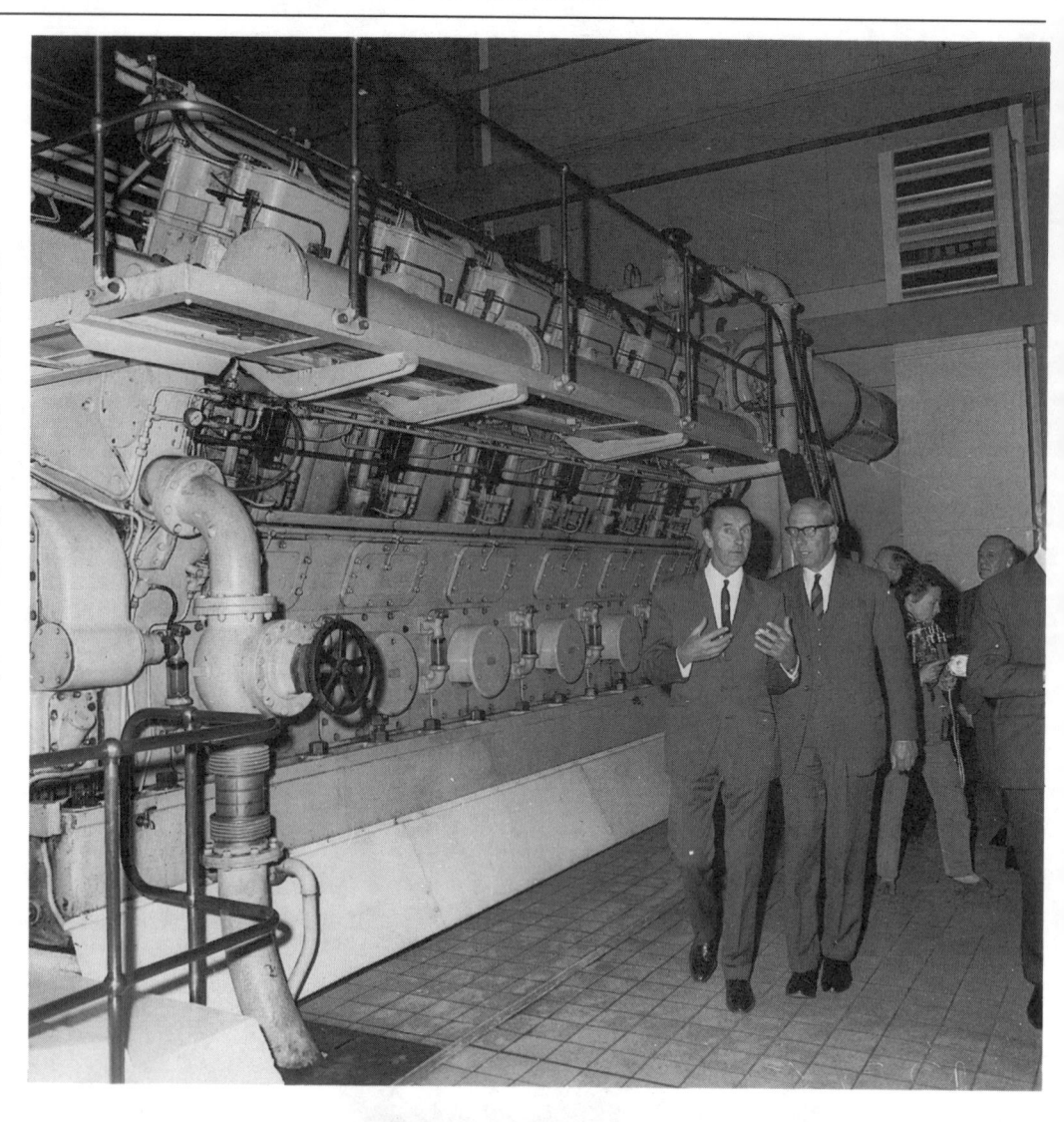

A man was jailed by the Magistrate's Court in June, although he had denied being the driver of a pick up truck that had crashed onto the deck of a gas tanker, moored in St Sampson's Harbour. The 22-year-old was convicted of stealing the vehicle, driving under the influence of drink and driving without third party insurance. He was fined on all charges, but said he had no money so took the jail term instead. The ship was loaded with 216 tons of butane gas at the time, so the emergency services were stood by, and householders in the area were evacuated.

A much-needed new block for inmates of the States prison was viewed by Lt-Governor Sir Charles Mills in January. The president of the Prison Board, Deputy H. C. Henchman, told an Evening Press reporter that the board had adopted the policy of keeping prisoners out of their cells for as long as possible - between 7am and 9pm every day - and as well as providing new cells, the new £21,000 block gave the men a recreation area for table tennis and darts. The new cells accommodated 19 prisoners, and the block had been built in the old recreation and work courtyard. There was also a new messroom. The cost of the building had been kept down by using prisoners to help construct the block, and the men were also responsible for making much of its furniture.

Britain goes decimal, ending pounds, shillings and pence. Switzerland allows women the vote.

1971

Geoffrey Rippon, the UK Government's chief Common Market negotiator, visited Guernsey in November to address the States on the terms he had negotiated. In a 26-minute address, Mr Rippon (standing next to the Bailiff, Sir William Arnold) described the terms as 'highly satisfactory'. The Advisory and Finance Committee said that non-entry would be disastrous and the States voted unanimously to support the committee's proposals in December. In doing so, they discounted a petition signed by 14,758 islanders opposed to Guernsey joining.

Guernsey, like Britain, switched over to decimal coinage on 15 February. This caused some bewilderment, particularly for elderly islanders, and complaints about immediate price rises brought about by the change to 100p in the pound.

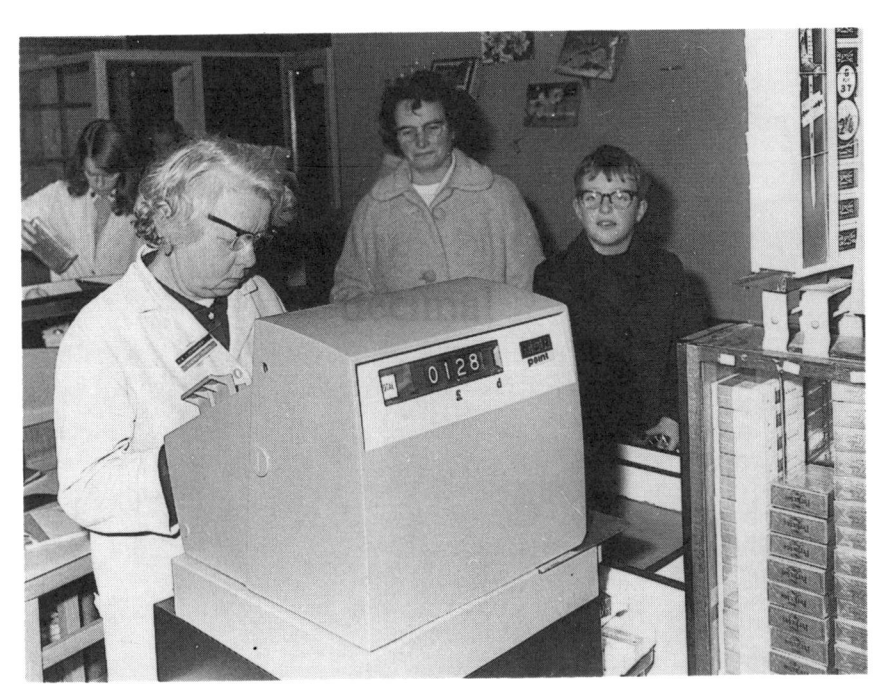

1971

First British soldier dies in Ulster. Campaign for Real Ale set up. Jim Morrison of The Doors dies in Paris.

A new telephone cable linking Guernsey with the UK came ashore at L'Ancresse (above).

With the postal service in chaos because of a national strike, Lt-Col Patrick Wootton (at the driving wheel), the tenant of Lihou, announced plans in March to expand his private postal service and link up with similar organisations in the UK to provide a strike beating service. But hoteliers rejected the system and a few days later the national strike was called off.

Aswan High Dam opens on the River Nile. Attica Prison riot quelled by US National Guard – 39 dead.

1971

109

Work on the new container berth was well under way, heralding in a new method of handling cargo entering and leaving the island.

All of the houses and flats in the massive Bouet development built by Maxim Construction were handed over to the Housing Authority.

1971

Three jailed for obscene 'Schoolkids' Issue' of underground magazine Oz. Taiwan expelled from UN to allow China in.

Tickets for the first States of Guernsey Lottery went on sale in June with a first prize of £3,000. A total of 27,000 tickets were issued and sold. Gambling Control Committee members Deputies Tony Bran and Iris Pouteaux attended the first draw to see the winning numbers drawn.

The Bailiff, Sir William Arnold, criticised the Water Board's failure to act quickly enough to avert the island's water crisis. The level of the St Saviour's reservoir dropped to its lowest level for many years with the old cottages revealed by the falling water.

End of the line for the Victorian barracks at Fort Le Marchant. Completed in 1854, the disused building was demolished when it became dangerous. The older, Napoleonic parts of the fort remain.

'Bloody Sunday' shootings in Belfast. Miners' strike blacks out Britain. First woman rabbi ordained in US.

1972

Last rites for St Paul's. The final demolition of St Paul's Methodist Church took place in March 1972. The site eventually became a sunken garden.

Hang on a minute, isn't this It's a Knockout? Guernsey took on Bournemouth in a special It's a Knockout challenge during the 1972 Summer Festival of Sport at Les Vauxbelets. An estimated 3,000 spectators watched Bournemouth win the event by two points.

1972

Black September terrorists kill 11 Israeli athletes at Munich Olympics. Earthquake destroys Managua, capital of Nicaragua.

Liner Queen Elizabeth destroyed by fire in Hong Kong Harbour. Britain joins EEC.

1972

113

The UK dockers' strike wreaked havoc with the local tomato industry in the summer of 1972 as these pictures show. During the month-long dispute more than 40,000 trays of tomatoes were dumped in Bordeaux Quarry which resembled a vast, muddy bowl of very pungent red soup. A mood of helpless resignation descended on the growing industry until Operation Red-Skin came into operation a fortnight into the dispute. The Tomato Marketing Board's emergency plan involved American Hercules freighters airlifting the fruit to the UK. In all the Hercules aircraft made 49 flights to the UK before the dockers returned to work.

1972

Watergate Hotel election headquarters break-in in US. First North Sea oil comes ashore.

The greeting was warm, the weather windy and wet, as Princess Anne arrived for her two-day visit to the Bailiwick. Hundreds of Guernsey people lined the streets of St Peter Port on 24 May to greet the Royal visitor, who was accompanied by Lt-Governor Sir John Mills and the Bailiff, Sir William Arnold. During her stay Princess Anne officially opened the new harbour container berth and visited Saumarez Park where residents of Longue Rue House had a privileged view of the Princess.

This monster 10lb lobster (above) was caught in 65ft of water south of the Castle Breakwater by diver John Barbe. The picture showing the enormity of the creature was taken prior to it being sold on to the Absolute End restaurant. The smaller lobster shown is an average sized 3- to 4-year-old.

West Indian Test batsman Gordon Greenidge and South African star Barry Richards walk out to bat for Hampshire at the College Field in the summer. Hampshire played three matches in the island that summer, one of which local all-rounder Pierre Le Cocq will always remember - he dismissed Greenidge for nought!

US ends bombing of Vietnam, ceasefire signed, troops pull out. First woman stockbroker on floor of London exchange.

1973

115

Protesters demonstrated outside the Royal Court before the States debate on whether or not Icart headland was to be used as a golf course. Their actions, and a 10,000-signature petition, meant that Frank Stroobant's working party recommendations were thrown out and Guernsey's second golf course was to be another 20 years in the making.

The Arab-Israeli war and subsequent cut in Arab oil supplies touched Guernsey and by the end of October the authorities were calling for caution in the use of hydrocarbon fuels. Growers said they could not cut back without fear of losing their crops. By December, electricity power supplies were cut back and petrol was being served a gallon at a time. Derrick Eury (right) and his daughter Helen were not worried about petrol rationing. Their one-donkey-power cart only needed carrots for fuel.

1973

American Indians end 10-week takeover of Wounded Knee. Forty six die in fire at Summerland leisure centre, Isle of Man.

On Christmas morning, probably Guernsey's biggest ever shipwreck, the Monrovian registered bulk carrier Elwood Mead, carrying 120,000 tons of iron from Australia to Rotterdam, struck Les Grunes Reef during her maiden voyage. It was two months before the huge vessel, lightened by having its cargo pumped overboard, could be dragged free by ocean going tugs.

Boats were in the news again in May, when the 9,600 ton freighter Captain Niko sank three miles off Rousse (above). Her cargo of bulk fertiliser had shifted in heavy seas and she sank despite the efforts of the supply ship Tender Turbot to tow her to safety. One seaman, an 18-year-old Egyptian, died when he was flung from a lifeboat when it fell from davits into the water.

A Royal Navy helicopter ferried ashore survivors of the shipwrecked Cypriot-registered cargo ship Armas (right) after she hit rocks off Burhou near Alderney. Ten crewmen tried to launch a lifeboat but the huge seas capsized the boat, throwing the men into the sea. One man, Pakistani Abdel La Tita, was swept away and drowned. Six of those rescued needed hospital attention.

Yom Kippur War – Israel routs invaders Egypt and Syria, US threatens world war unless USSR stops supplying arms to Arabs.

1973

117

In the 11 October edition of the Evening Press Kate Green interviewed the man who probably had more influence on the island's property market than any other, speculator Ernest Wolfgang Brauch. At the time it was said he owned £10m.-worth of island bricks and mortar including eight hotels, two guest houses, Beaucette marina, the zoo, the Iron Stores building, numerous open market houses, High Street shops, and 12 local market houses. His empire was to collapse as property prices fell, and it was as a direct result of his activities that the island's law was changed to bring in the Dwellings Profits Tax Law against short term speculation in property.

The first Olde **Guernsey Market opened** with glorious **sunshine and thronging** crowds on **29 June. It is still a tourist** attraction.

1973

Oil producers blackmail West, impose 70% price hike. Sydney Opera House opens.

John Henry Loveridge (left) was sworn in as Bailiff in the Royal Court. Mr Loveridge (later Sir John) had qualified as an advocate, became a legislative draftsman and was attached to the staff of the Parliamentary Counsel in London before being appointed Guernsey's HM Comptroller in 1954. He became HM Procureur six years later.

Within three days of arriving in Guernsey, the new lifeboat, Sir William Arnold, was called into action when the 55ft yacht Lord Trenchard, crewed by 10 RAF personnel, snapped her mainmast (right).

October started with the usual storms and the lifeboat was launched to stand by the Spanish ship Monola Toro which had developed a list to starboard in heavy seas. The same front page recorded that two cows standing 100 yards apart on Mr Peter Hocart's farm in St Andrew's had been killed by one stroke of lightning.

A record number of visitors were forecast and with a boom in boating in evidence, the Old Harbour (left) was converted into the Victoria Marina by the simple expedient of building a low wall across the harbour mouth and installing pontoons.

Japanese World War Two soldier found on Lubang, Philippines. Princess Anne shot at in kidnap attempt.

1974

119

The States agreed after an eight-hour debate on 24 April to go ahead with the development of a sports and leisure centre at Beau Sejour. The following day the House agreed to save the former church of St James the Less and convert this to a concert and assembly hall. The Save St James campaigners were outside the States building to emphasise their point as members went in.

Islanders were forced to adopt various energy saving methods when the island was plunged into crisis in the early months of the year. The Emergency Council threatened petrol rationing and a ban on Sunday motoring as ways of saving precious resources. Motor sport was banned, but the resourceful members of the Motor Cycle and Car Club held cyclotests rather than car tests and held a table top rally. All restrictions were lifted in early March.

1974

Turkish Airlines' DC10 crashes near Paris, killing 344. Lord Lucan disappears after murder of nanny.

The 2,000 ton Cypriot cargo ship Prosperity was wrecked on La Conchee Reef off Perelle during the stormy night of 17 January with the loss of all 18 crew members. The ship's cargo of timber was strewn along the west and south coast. Much of it was salvaged, some of it unofficially. The seven Moslem crew members on board were buried in a communal grave at the Foulon Cemetery. The crew members are remembered on a memorial which was paid for by public subscription. The wreck of the ship lay within a few miles of the massive bulk carrier Elwood Mead, which was pulled clear of Les Grunes Reef on 24 February, two months after it had run aground.

1974

West German chancellor Willy Brandt resigns after East German spy found in his staff. Richard Nixon quits as US president.

1974

Covent Garden fruit and vegetable market closes. Russian ballet dancer Mikhail Baryshnikov defects to the West.

Clarrie and Alice Blondel (left) were proud people on 30 March when two of their sons and two of their nephews represented Guernsey at football on the same day. Ray and Peter Blondel, their sons, were in the Guernsey team which beat Alderney in the Muratti semi-final, while Kevin and Carl Le Tissier were in the winning Star Trophy schoolboy team.

The Duchess of Kent visited the island in May to name the island's new Arun class lifeboat Sir William Arnold (right) and to open the old folks home which bears her name.

The Lt-Governor, Sir Charles Mills, left Guernsey in August when his term of office expired (below). His successor, Sir John Martin, arrived in the island in October.

This house in La Mazotte, Vale, was destroyed when a gas explosion ripped through it at night.

Organisation of Petroleum Exporting Countries raises crude prices again. Charlie Chaplin knighted.

1975

A sure sign of a long, hot and dry summer in Guernsey is the re-appearance of the farm buildings submerged when St Saviour's reservoir was completed in 1947. The farm shown was one of seven lost to quench the thirst of the Guernsey public.

Ready to take on the world: Miss Guernsey, 17-year-old Carol Le Billon, lined up alongside the world's most attractive women in the annual Miss World competition in London.

1975

Baader Meinhof terrorists go on trial in Stuttgart. North Sea oil starts to flow.

Fifteen years after making her first cross-Channel run the mailboat Caesarea (above) leaves Guernsey waters for the last time.

Down she goes: Les Touillets Tower, built by the Germans, is demolished to be replaced by a television mast.

Angola gains independence from Portugal. Margaret Thatcher becomes Conservative leader.

1975

The new Arun lifeboat 54-03 was in Guernsey for comparison trials with the Sir William Arnold when the 10,000-ton Pegase (above) reported being on fire 15 miles north-west of Guernsey on February 27. The crew abandoned ship before the two lifeboats arrived and were picked up by the mv Christian Matherson. The aircraft carrier HMS Hermes sent a helicopter with a doctor to treat one seaman suffering from serious burns. One man was missing and the Sir William Arnold searched without success while 54-03 ferried 20 crew to Guernsey. Four crew returned to Pegase to await a salvage tug. They can be seen this side of the hatch cover nearest the bow.

When the tanker Point Law (right) ran aground at the base of cliffs in Alderney the lifeboat Sir William Arnold was sent to help. A French helicopter winched a man from the stern of the stricken tanker. The discoloured sea marks the escape of oil from the tanks.

1975

Moorgate tube disaster kills 35. Chinese unearth terracotta army at Xi'an. Civil war starts in Beirut.

Queen Elizabeth, the Queen Mother, paid another welcome visit and, among many engagements, met local schoolchildren and teachers. At the opening of La Mare de Carteret School headmaster Allan Gray is presented to Her Majesty.

Israeli commandos end hijack at Entebbe, freeing 98 hostages. Death of Viscount Montgomery of Alamein.

1976

The irrepressible Jimmy Savile played the pied piper as he led a gang of charity walkers from the White Rock to the Bridge and back to raise money for the Variety Club.

Unlucky for some! The island's emergency services dealt with six road accidents in an hour late in the evening of Friday 13 February. The most spectacular was this three-car crash in the Rue du Dos D'Ane, Castel, where all three vehicles were blazing wrecks. All the drivers and passengers escaped serious injury.

1976

Mary Langdon becomes first UK woman fireman. Britain seeks help from International Monetary Fund.

1976 will long be remembered as the year of the drought. As early as May the Water Board were asking for a state of emergency to be called. Restrictions on water use were tough as islanders saved every drop. The drought came to a spectacular end in September, when five months' rain fell in three days, and the reservoir was overflowing by the end of the year.

Fire swept the island's south coast one weekend at the end of August in one of the worst cliff fires in living memory. Flames up to 40ft consumed vast areas of undergrowth and firemen and volunteers fought the fire bravely over two days.

Guatamala earthquake kills 22,000. Poison cloud of dioxin covers Seveso, northern Italy. American spacecraft lands on Mars.

1976

Alderney's hopes of marking their first-ever Muratti match on home soil with a victory were dashed when Guernsey beat the northern isle 5-0 at the Mount Hale pitch. The match drew a crowd of some 500 people.

Prince Charles paid his first official visit to Guernsey in May 1976 as commanding officer of the minesweeper HMS Bronington. He spent three days in the island, and returned for an unscheduled visit later in the year.

1976

Iceland severs diplomatic relations with UK over Cod War. Vietnam reunified. Race ace Nikki Lauda escapes death in crash.

Beau Sejour Leisure Centre opened for business in December (above), attracting 8,500 on a weekend when the centre first opened for people to take a look around. The centre, some 10 years in the planning, cost about £2m. to build.

With the island's new leisure centre under construction in the background, Beau Sejour House (right), the 19th century building that was the offices for three States committees, was demolished at the beginning of the year.

Candie auditorium (left), venue for many famous concerts over the years, was demolished at the beginning of the year to make way for the island's purpose-built museum.

Trade unions legalised in Spain for first time since 1936. Silver Jubilee of Queen Elizabeth II.

1977

131

The British Rail's Sarnia said goodbye with a final sailing on Saturday 10 September. A volunteer band from HMS Heron played from the top deck of the mailboat which came into service, after being named by Lady Arnold, in June 1961. It was replaced by the car ferry Earl Godwin.

A 763-ton freighter hit and became trapped on rocks off the north-east side of the Grande Braye, off the northern tip of Guernsey on the night of Tuesday 18 January. Within an hour of leaving St Peter Port the Owenglas became lodged on the rocks and had to wait to be freed by a rising tide. The lifeboat and the ambulance boat stood by but the ship did not take in any water and the crew stayed on board. It floated free at 3.15 the next morning.

1977

Two jumbo jets collide at Tenerife, killing 574. Red Rum wins hat trick Grand National.

These two penguins hit the front page in March when they disappeared just two days after arriving at Guernsey zoo. The tiny South American birds, which cannot fly, had settled in happily but vanished during the night from their six foot high pen. A taxi driver found them the next day walking unharmed along the Forest Road.

Hundreds of islanders went ormering in icy waters when a three-year ban was lifted on 19 January. Despite the respite for the local delicacy, catches were light and most of them were older ormers which seemed to show that stocks did not recover during the ban. One man at Rousse said he had to go up to his waist in water to get a dozen ormers. 'It was hardly worth the trouble,' he said. On the two low tides of 19th and 20th about 30,000 ormers were gathered and were selling for £4.20 a dozen in the market. Rocquaine, pictured here, was one of the more popular places.

Elvis Presley dies. Freddie Laker's Skytrain flies to New York.

1977

Guernsey's first charity swimarathon made a big splash with 200 teams taking part in the event at Beau Sejour which was arranged by the Lions Club, Round Table, and Variety Club. Of the thousand or so swimmers who took part three celebrities also took the plunge - Oliver Reed, television star Philip Madoc, and British swimmer Brian Brinkley.

Town residents were entertained by an enthusiastic group of young folk singers who combined carol singing with raising money for a mobile library. Judy Beaugeard, now better known as a St Peter Port deputy, led the folk group around the town and collected money for the Books for Children Group.

1977

Passengers freed from Mogadishu hijack.
Marc Bolan of T Rex dies in car crash.

The Bailiwick joined communities across the UK to celebrate The Queen's Silver Jubilee with the lighting of a bonfire at Vale Castle. Deputy Bailiff Charles Frossard lit Guernsey's beacon, which was one in a chain of a hundred across the kingdom on the night of 6 June, at 10.37pm. There were three hearty cheers from the huge crowd and the simple ceremony passed without hitch. There were also fires burning in Alderney, Herm, Sark, and Lihou. The next day the Bailiwick's jubilee celebrations began with a Thanksgiving Service at the Town Church and a 21-gun salute from Castle Cornet, a cavalcade, a spectacular tableau and dancing displays at Cambridge Park and sports events at Beau Sejour. The day drew to a close with a massive street party in St Peter Port and a firework display. Souvenirs included a special issue of the Evening Press and a mug to every school child.

Monday 9 May was a bad day for local sport when Guernsey suffered a punishing defeat to Jersey in the 61st Muratti. The green and whites lost 5-1, the worst home defeat for 51 years. There was one moment of glory, pictured here, when Peter Blondel scored his goal.

First test tube baby born. Bulgarian defector Georgi Markov stabbed with poison umbrella tip in London.

1978

Ten million pounds worth of oil rig crashed ashore on the west coast one stormy February night. Thirty three men were plucked to safety by the St Peter Port lifeboat and Royal Navy helicopters. The 19,000-ton rig Orion, mounted on a giant barge, broke away from its towing tug. The relief St Peter Port lifeboat, John Gellatly Hyndman, managed to pluck some of the crew off the rig before it came ashore at Grandes Rocques headland. The Navy helicopters came in under low cloud and hovered perilously close to the legs of the jack-up rig and lifted more of the crew to safety, despite the rig swinging through 180 degrees. As the tide fell the rest of the crew were considered safe on the rig and stayed there until the lifeboat could take them off next morning. Hundreds of islanders watched the daring rescue from the headland. A massive salvage operation was mounted by the Dutch firm Wijsmuller, which had rescued the Elwood Mead from the Les Grunes Reef just offshore some four years earlier, yet it was weeks before the rig could be floated from the barge and towed away. The barge Federal 400-2 was eventually towed away for repair.

1978

Supertanker Amoco Cadiz runs aground off Brittany. Punk rocker Sid Vicious charged with murder in New York.

When the supertanker Amoco Cadiz broke up 110 miles away off the coast of Brittany in March hundreds of thousands of gallons of oil were released into the sea and started drifting towards the island. A massive clean-up swung into action with a fleet of oil dispersant tugs based in St Peter Port, and for days the air was heavy with crude oil fumes. Some oil came ashore in Guernsey and considerable efforts had to be made to clean it up. Here samples are taken at Petit Bot.

The year started with a bang. Gales whipped the island causing widespread damage. Two occupants of this Vazon cottage had a lucky escape when the wind tore off part of the roof.

Birching remained on the island's statute book in 1978 but the European Court decided that it was a degrading punishment following an appeal from the Isle of Man. The birch was last used in Guernsey four years earlier.

Red Brigade kidnap Italian prime minister Aldo Moro, then kill him. Sweden bans aerosols.

1978

137

June saw a visit by The Queen and the Duke of Edinburgh aboard the royal yacht Britannia. Her Majesty spent a day in Guernsey and the following day visited both Sark and Alderney. Thousands turned out to see The Queen during her two walkabouts of the day and she was inundated with gifts of flowers (above). She passed through the crowd in Church Square on her way to the Market. Another walkabout marked Her Majesty's trip to Alderney. There she was escorted by the Lt-Governor, Vice Admiral Sir John Martin.

138 **1978** Israel and Egypt reach peace agreement. Charlie Chaplin's coffin stolen in Switzerland.

St John Ambulance's cliff rescue service saved an 11 year-old boy from cliffs above Telegraph Bay in August. Sean Goddard and his friend David Trether were climbing on the cliff when they became trapped. Ambulanceman Neil Tucker, later to become chief officer of the Ambulance and Rescue Service, made his way down the dangerous cliff to rescue the trapped boy whose friend was rescued by other ambulancemen who reached him from the beach.

Five thousand people were fed in four hours (right) when a whole ox was spit roast in Saumarez Park during a Variety Club function. Dairy Committee president Bob Chilcott was on hand to carve the first slice.

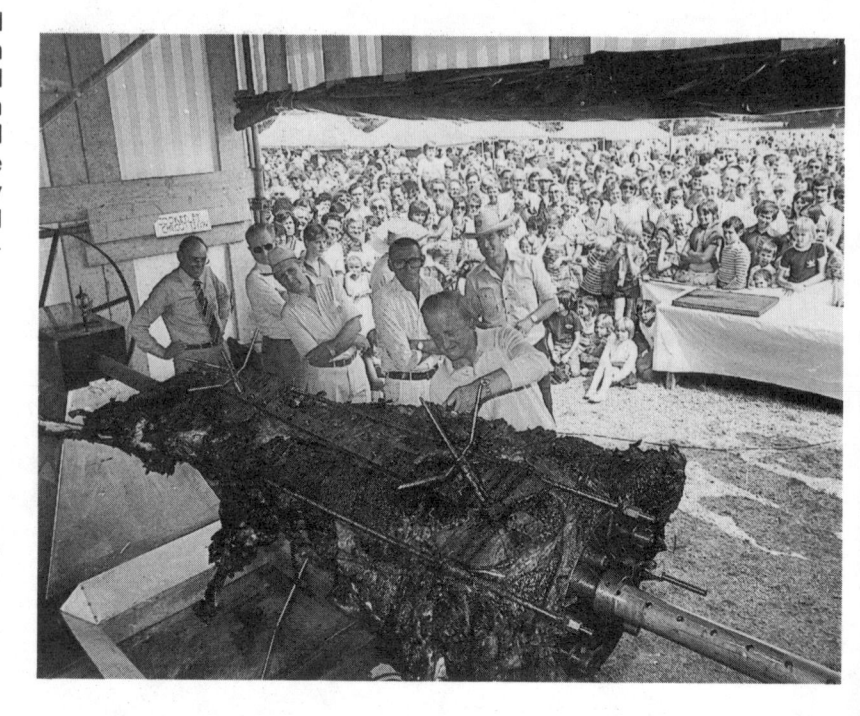

'Crisis? What crisis?' asks Labour prime minister James Callaghan as hundreds of thousands of workers are laid off by strikes.

1979

It was a sad day when the brothers of Les Vauxbelets (above) quit dairy farming and auctioned off their high quality cows and heifers for a combined total of £2,675.

The Guernsey Museum and Art Gallery (right) beat 33 other national establishments to win the coveted Illustrated London News' Museum of the Year Award. The judges said it was a model of what a 'small and excellent' museum should be. The award – £2,000 and a porcelain sculpture by Henry Moore – was presented to the museum curator Rona Cole at a special lunch in London.

Return of the Luftwaffe (left). A Fokker VFW 614 jet stands at Guernsey airport, the first time an aircraft of the German Air Force had landed in the island for 34 years.

140   **1979**   Kmer Rouge genocide exposed in Cambodia. Margaret Thatcher is Britain's first woman prime minister.

September 1979 and Operation Tom Dumping (above) was in full swing as British housewives showed little interest in buying the fruit. It was estimated 40 lorry loads a day were being dumped in Bordeaux Quarry, much of it in perfect condition. The dumped toms were simply too big or too small for inclusion in the pink and white grades being transported at the time.

Radio and TV celebrity Jimmy Savile 'fixed it' for many of his fans during a charity visit to the island in the summer. He raised money for the Variety Club by jogging around the Track 50 times in less than two hours (left).

Three Mile Island nuclear reactor leak in US. Dictator Idi Amin flees Uganda. First cycle plane crossing of the Channel.

1979

141

Rock superstars Status Quo warmed up for their 1979 world tour with a memorable one-nighter at Beau Sejour. More than 1,500 local rock fans heard the supergroup perform for two pulsating and ear-bashing hours. The group's equipment was brought to Guernsey in three 32-ton pantechnicons, so large that they could not be driven on Guernsey roads and had to be offloaded at the White Rock.

Those experts in daredevil flying – the RAF's Red Arrows – were back in Town, or should it be over it! John Brenton's picture shows one of the Gnat aircraft hurtling over a packed harbour.

Photographers and TV film crews swarm over every vantage point to get a sight of the action at the first ever all First Division soccer match played in Guernsey. Birmingham City and West Bromwich Albion drew 1-1 in the friendly watched by more than 3,000 spectators at Blanche Pierre Lane.

1979

Concorde begins trans-Atlantic service. Shah leaves Iran, Ayatollah Khomeini takes power. IRA murder Lord Mountbatten.

A 75-year printing tradition ended on 3 November, 1979, (above) when publication of the Guernsey Evening Press and Star transferred from Smith Street, St Peter Port, to its present home at Braye Road. The paper, which began life in 1897 in the Pollet, moved to Smith Street in 1904.

Local fisherman Graham Eker (far left) caught more than he bargained for when he and his fellow crew members aboard the potter Press On discovered this propeller of a Second World War bomber tangled in their lobster pots off the coast of Guernsey.

Pirate radio ship Caroline sinks. Death of Grand Admiral Karl Doenitz, briefly Fuhrer in 1945. Start of Iran-Iraq war.

1980

143

An unusual haul was landed by Customs in June when one and a quarter tons of cannabis was discovered on the yacht Anntoo. It was the biggest haul of cannabis resin ever found here and was revealed when customs took apart the 40ft vessel. The haul was valued at £2m.

1980

SAS storm Iranian embassy in London to free hostages – live on TV. Mount St Helens volcano explodes.

The macabre problem of what to do with bodies which were in the way of plans to establish a new reservoir at St Sampson's, occupied local authorities at the start of the year. It was decided that 2,000 remains would be exhumed. Relatives and church organisers listened as Water Board staff explained the pressing need to develop Longue Hougue as a reservoir.

A new Lt-Governor took his oath of office in April. Air Chief Marshal Sir Peter Le Cheminant spoke to a crowded Royal Court House in patois. He promised the gathering that he would do everything possible for Guernsey. Sir Peter was welcomed by Bailiff Sir John Loveridge 'as one Guernseyman to another'.

America's attempt to free 53 Teheran embassy hostages fails as rescuers crash in desert. John Lennon shot dead in New York.

1980

145

The first air search service which has become an accepted addition to the emergency services was acquired in January. The twin engined Piper Aztec, crewed by volunteers, was available whenever St John Ambulance or the lifeboat required aerial assistance. It was welcomed by the rescue services who saw it as a valuable addition.

A hay storm was reported in August when St Peter's parishioners found themselves covered in a sudden downpour of dried grass. The hay landed on rooftops, glasshouses and neatly kept lawns and was thought to have been whipped up by rising hot air. Bewildered islanders were amazed to see clumps of hay on telephone wires and poles.

1980

Mine lift cage plunges a mile in South African gold mine, killing 23. Polish shipyard workers take over yard at Gdansk.

The former Vimiera College was demolished to make way for the luxurious St Pierre Park Hotel. The 35-acre site was cleared and building began in the autumn. Thought had been given to converting the college building but this was ruled out because of the extent of its neglect.

One of the greenest spots in the island was discovered to be at risk in May when the former L'Eree airfield went up for sale. States members discovered that the area was being offered with permission for more than 100 houses. A successful campaign was launched to ensure it remained a valuable green oasis.

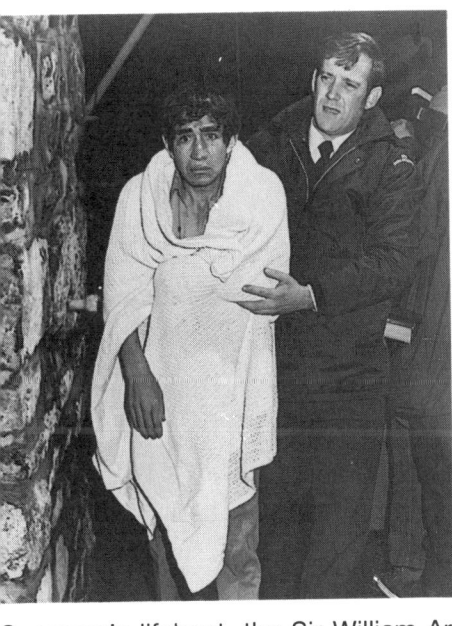

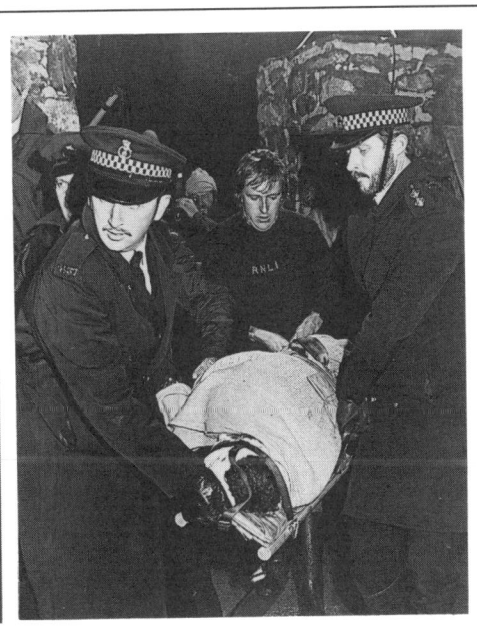

Millions of strikers bring Poland to a halt. Shergar wins the Derby. Israel bombs Iraqi reactor.

1981

147

Guernsey's lifeboat, the Sir William Arnold, rescued 29 people from a stricken freighter in danger of sinking in a dramatic three hour rescue in December. The 10,000 ton freighter Bonita was caught in hurricane force winds which left the ship listing badly. Helicopters winched five of the Bonita's crew to safety, a French tug rescued another and one man died during the incident. It was the first major operation for the lifeboat's recently-appointed coxswain, Mike Scales - at the time one of the youngest lifeboatmen in Britain. The crew of the Bonita who were taken on board the lifeboat were landed at Brixham in the UK. During the rescue, the lifeboat made 50 runs to the stern of the sinking ship before putting in to Brixham itself to allow the crew to rest before heading home. As the lifeboat arrived in St Peter Port, the Signal Station flew international code flags bearing a simple message: "Welcome home." There was a personal greeting from Lt-Governor Sir Peter Le Cheminant and his wife.

1981

Prince Charles marries Lady Diana Spencer. £45m. in gold raised from HMS Edinburgh, sunk in Barents Sea in May 1942.

Archaeology hit the headlines in the early months of the year, with islanders and archaeologists alike getting excited over the excavation of a tomb at Les Fouaillages, L'Ancresse. For the first time in nearly 5,000 years, men entered the stone chambers of this burial mound and although bones were not found, it was thought that they had decomposed rapidly due to high soil acidity. But the most exciting finds were of arrowheads, pottery and masonry - the latter the oldest proven stonemasonry in the world. It took the team of diggers 12 weeks during three seasons to peel away the layers of the mound, to reveal the earliest traces of man in Guernsey - dating back some 7,000 years. There was plenty to get excited about, with an enthusiastic team of local helpers assisting the professionals on this delve into the island's distant past.

Opening of the Guille Alles Library in the Hayward Room after completion of a massive renovation programme for the huge building. The project was made possible through the generosity of former Jethou tenant Sir Charles Hayward.

Mehmet Ali Agca shoots Pope in Rome, Pope lives and forgives. Riots in Brixton.

1981

149

The crash landing of a Jersey European Airways Islander on the evening of Friday, 18 September, was probably one of the most remarkable locally. Miraculously, nobody was killed or even seriously injured when Captain Malcolm Le Moignan was forced to land in a field at La Brigade Road, St Andrew's, crashing into the gateway of La Brigade Farm Guest House. Although the passengers were clearly shaken, rumour had it that one man who did not live far away picked up his suitcase and walked home! One couple had their six month old daugther with them, and she, too, suffered only minor injuries in the crash. The pilot was praised by the passengers for managing to land without hitting any houses. This was one occasion where the incredible photographs pretty much told the story themselves.

One of Alderney's hotels came to a fiery end in March. The Grand Island Hotel was reduced to a pile of rubble in a huge blaze in the early hours of 20 March. Both the regular firemen and their colleagues from the island's airport were called in, but by the time they arrived on the scene it was too late. Strong winds had fanned the flames, and the hotel and its predominantly wooden chalets burned like tinder. At one point the heat was so intense that tarmac on the road nearby caught fire. Fortunately, the building was empty and there were no injuries. Most of the hotel's gas cylinders were removed, but two had to be left and added to the blaze when they exploded. A large part of the firemen's job was to stop the fire spreading to nearby properties and a large oil storage tank in the hotel grounds. The island's leading holiday hotel had stood for some 50 years so the tourist industry stood to be seriously affected by its loss. Police were suspicious as to the cause of the blaze, since the previous month there had been an incident elsewhere in the island where fuel had been poured through the letter box of a local shop and set alight.

1981

'Yorkshire Ripper' Peter Sutcliffe found guilty of 13 murders. Ronald Reagan becomes oldest US president.

The fear that Guernsey would suffer an outbreak of foot and mouth disease led to the island authorities taking what precautions they could to prevent its spread. The worry started when the killer disease was found in Jersey, and six cows and a bull were destroyed. It was thought that because of the way the disease spreads, Guernsey was at great risk. The disease had spread from France, carried on thermal currents on the air, and could also be spread by people who had been in an infected area. As a result, passengers at the airport and the docks found themselves having to walk on disinfectant trays as they disembarked, cars had their wheels sprayed as they left the ro-ro ferry, the Riding and Hunt Club cancelled their events and dog owners anticipated that all movement of their animals between the islands would be stopped. In Alderney a loudspeaker van toured the island, warning islanders to keep their dogs on leads and not to visit farmland, and all Sark farmers were told of the threat by the Agriculture Committee.

The news that the States had voted to demolish the Odeon Cinema marked the end of an era for local film fans. By a margin of just two votes, members put the idea of new States offices being built on the site ahead of retaining the unique cinema building, and decided that it would be razed. A petition from islanders was not enough to sway members towards keeping the building, and it was argued that it would prove too expensive to convert it to a concert hall, which was one idea put forward. Ultimately, it was demolished, the States changed their minds over the location of the new offices, and all the island got out of the demolition was a car park.

The start of the 1980s marked the onset of a new fad that appeared to signal a new era in communications - but it was not to be. Citizen Band radio came to the UK from the USA, where truckers had turned the use of two way radios in their cabs into a sub-culture, complete with its own bizarre language that ensured "outsiders" were kept at arms length, since anyone unfamiliar with the expressions used would wonder what on earth was being talked about. CB shops sprang up everywhere, and although there were question marks of the legality of the system locally (a licence had to be obtained), there was no shortage of islanders who were keen to stick an aerial on their car roof and drive around chatting to their friends. In an effort to make rather more practical use of the concept, a group of locals got together and formed Radio Emergency Associated Citizens Teams (React) to monitor the CB emergency band and help the emergency services. It was a brave attempt to give credibility to what many non-CB users saw as a passing craze - and were proved right when, as fast as it took off, interest died, leaving only a few die-hards and frequent road users on the air.

Falklands War after Argentina invades islands, British task force ejects the invaders by force.

1982

151

Home from the war. A happy and very relieved 19-year-old Steve Le Mesurier, radio operator on HMS Alacrity during the Falklands War, is met by relatives and friends on his return to Guernsey.

Drilling and excavating at North Beach to determine the extent of work needed for the proposed marina development.

1982

Queen woken by intruder sitting on her bed in Buckingham Palace. Anti cruise missile protest by Greenham Common women.

The beginning of an end of an era: The Odeon Cinema is seen in the early part of its demolition in the spring of 1982. The purpose-built cinema had opened in the late 1930s but was soon to be flattened and made into a car park!

Fisherman Herbie Nicols unfurls the Union Jack on La Grosse Rocque to continue a ceremony started 50 years earlier by another Cobo resident, Fred Martel. Before the war the flag was raised each August Bank Holiday, but since 1948 it has been raised on Liberation Day. The stormy west coast weather conditions quickly take their toll on the flags and it is rare for them to last more than a few months.

Tony Jacklin, one of Britain's all-time best golfers, performs a 'swinging adaptation' of the ancient topping out ceremony on the roof of the semi-built new St Pierre Park Hotel. Jacklin designed the nine-hole golf course which forms part of the hotel.

Air Florida jet plunges into Potomac River, Washington, killing 78, some survivors pulled from icy river - live on TV.

1982

153

More than 3,000 people packed into the Royal Festival Hall in London to see Guernsey lifeboatmen receive bravery medals from Princess Alice, the Duchess of Gloucester, for their part in the rescuing of 29 people from the stricken freighter Bonita in hurricane conditions last December. The eight were coxswain Mike Scales (far right, above, and right), who collected a gold medal (the lifeboatmen's VC), Peter Bougourd, Robert Vowles, John Webster, John Bougourd, Peter Bisson, Richard Hamon and Alan Martel, who received bronze medals.

154 1982 Italian banker Robert Calvi found hanging under Blackfriars Bridge, London. US marines sent to Beirut after massacre.

It is not New Zealand yet there are kiwis everywhere: John and Gunilla Hailes, of Fernvale Plants Ltd, Les Effards, St Sampson's, and John Lacey, of Willit Vinery, Vale, gambled their future on the 'pleasing tropical taste' of the kiwifruit.

On air: Radio Guernsey officially opened on Tuesday, 16 March, 1982. The ceremony was conducted by the Bailiff, Sir John Loveridge, in the presence of George Howard, chairman of the BBC board of governors.

BBC pioneers breakfast TV. Klaus Barbie goes on trial for war crimes in Lyon, France. First cordless phones in Britain.

1983

155

Yob culture: Police made more than 50 arrests and quelled trouble as Guernsey and Jersey yobs clashed on Muratti final day. Youths fought running battles after the match which Guernsey won 2-1 at the Track. The pictures were taken at the White Rock where 20 police and two police dogs formed a cordon at the entrance to the harbour and came under attack from stones, eggs, coins and bricks.

156 1983 Racehorse Shergar kidnapped in Ireland.
'Fourth man' spy Anthony Blunt dies.

Hot shot Charles Trotter is met by his wife at Guernsey Airport on his return from Brisbane in Australia where he won a bronze medal in the full bore shooting event. At the same Games fellow Guernseyman Matthew Guille won a silver medal in the air rifle competition, the first ever medal won by a Sarnian at the Commonwealth Games.

Car bomb destroys US embassy in Beirut. Russians shoot down Korean Airlines jumbo jet, killing 269.

1983

157

Daredevil rider Eddie Kidd jumps through a blazing wall as part of his exhibition in front of 1,000 spectators at Foote's Lane.

Come in the environmentalists: October 1983 saw Dave Fletcher and Ron Le Moignan become the first deputies to be elected on an environmental ticket. The two were swept into office in the island's 'mini' elections of that year. Our picture shows Dave Fletcher receiving congratulations from friends after his overwhelming win in the St Peter Port election.

1983

Australia wins America's Cup. US marines invade Grenada. £25m. Brinks-Mat bullion robbery in UK.

Where's the sand gone? A sunny September day at Cobo Bay but the beach is barely recognisable after late summer storms dumped tons of vraic on the beaches.

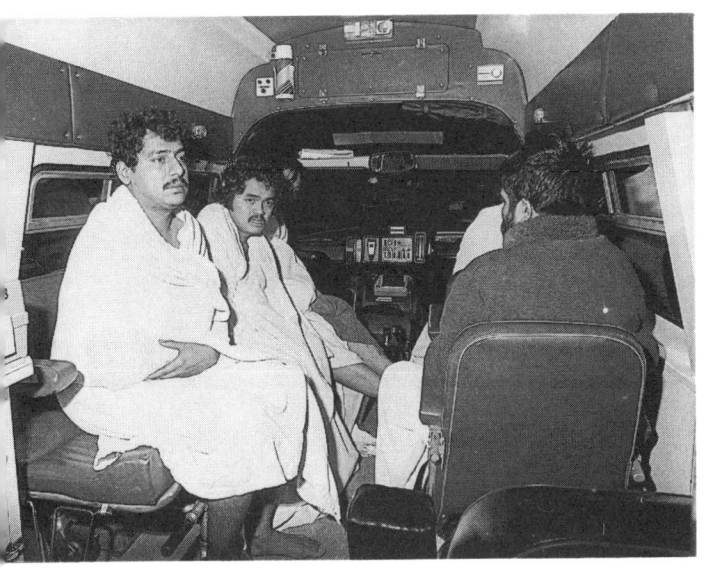

Torvill and Dean win ice skating gold at Sarajevo. Marvin Gaye shot by his father.

1984

159

Survivors from the Liberian grain carrier, Radiant Med, which sank some 14 miles off St Martin's Point early on 25 January are brought ashore. Only nine of the 25 crew members survived. The drama started at about 11pm the previous evening when the Radiant Med sent out a Mayday call for help. She was ploughing through rough seas off Les Roches Douvres, some miles off St Martin's point. Water was being taken into her hold and she was developing a 25 degree list. A French warship, the Casablanca, was nearby and her captain answered the call for help. Arriving on the scene, the warship started to escort the listing vessel to Cherbourg. With more water being taken aboard the grain carrier, the French rescue services asked that the St Peter Port lifeboat be sent to the scene. Then came the message that the listing ship was partly submerged and some of the crew were in the water. The Guernsey lifeboat, the Sir William Arnold, arrived on the scene at 3.20am, where they pulled nine seamen out of a lifeboat which was awash. A tenth man who was wedged in the ship's boat was dead, and his body had to be abandoned. Following an extensive air and sea search, fourteen bodies were accounted for, with a further two still missing, believed to have gone down with the ship. The ship's log, radio log and medical certificates of those who perished were found tied around the neck of one of the bodies. The survivors were taken to hospital, and later sent out a message of thanks to their saviours, saying: 'Tell the people of Guernsey we owe our lives to your lifeboat.'

1984

IRA bomb government at Grand Hotel, Brighton, narrowly missing Prime Minister Margaret Thatcher.

The Little Theatre and Renoir's night club, at Clifton steps, St Peter Port, are destroyed by fire in the early hours of the morning. The fire was one of the biggest Guernsey had ever seen, and neighbours had to be taken to the police station until the danger had passed. The following afternoon there were pockets of fire still smouldering in the ruins of the disco. Although it was at first believed that the blaze was started by a 'person of persons unknown', no one was ever convicted.

The end of a popular entertainment centre in St Peter Port. The Cellar Club and a number of other old properties at the upper part of Le Truchot, St Peter Port, are demolished to make room for new office accommodation.

Lightning causes fire which destroys part of York Minster. 3,000 Indians die in Bhopal pesticide plant spill.

1984

Sea fisheries officer John Lintell comes up for a breath of air (above), clutching a good-sized ormer taken from shallow water on the south of Lihou Island.

The Queen Mother makes her fourth visit to Guernsey (below). Hundreds of islanders and tourists cram into Church Square, St Peter Port, to catch a glimpse of the great lady and present her with posies and bouquets. The day opened in glorious sunshine and ended with a show of technicolour in the form of a magnificent firework display over Castle Cornet.

Acclaimed actor and part-time Guernsey resident Oliver Reed steps into the limelight of the island's Magistrate's Court. The public gallery was full with locals, visitors and media representatives who had got wind of Mr Reed's arrest. He was fined a total of £100 for damaging a hotel window and acting in a disorderly manner while dressed only in his underpants. Mr Reed left the island soon after the court case to do some work on his latest film – but not before fitting in a swift pint at one of the local pubs.

162　　　　1984　　　　Civil servant Sarah Tisdall jailed for leaking cruise missile story to Guardian.

The wreck of a Roman galley found between the St Peter Port pierheads prompts world-wide interest from archaeologists and historians on the discovery that it pre-dates any other wooden wreck in the sea in the UK by 1,000 years. The 20-metre ship was first discovered by professional diver Richard Keen in 1982. Marine archaeologist Margaret Rule, famous for leading the raising of the Mary Rose, was among those to visit the island to examine the wreck.

Work is under way on the development of the North Beach scheme to create a new marina and car park. Clearly seen are the huge concrete steps built up to road level. These formed a hard standing for the crane used to place sections of the sliced blockwork wall for the South Quay.

Clive Sinclair launches ill-fated C5 bike. UK coal miners' strike reaches bitter end after nearly a year.

1985

163

The first full assembly at the new co-educational Grammar School was held in September. Most pupils were at the school last term, but it was not until the autumn that the school was fully occupied.

In March the States approved a flag for Guernsey designed by Commander Bruce Nicolls. This showed the red cross of St George with the gold cross of William the Conqueror superimposed on it.

1985

Bradford football ground fire kills 40.
Skeleton said to be Auschwitz war criminal
Dr Joseph Mengele found in Brazil.

Mrs Donnie Le Pelley became the island's first woman jurat in October, a position held by her late husband, Jean.

Work on the new marina at North Beach was well under way by the summer. Here the rubble and pre-cast walls are about to meet, forming the area which, after infilling with silt dredged from the harbour, would become the Salerie car park.

1985

AIDS proclaimed a world-wide epidemic.
Earthquake destroys much of Mexico City.
Air India jumbo jet explodes over Atlantic.

The coaster Corinna ran aground on the Brimtides Reef off the Alderney coast in February. The six crew waited until the tide dropped to walk ashore from the stricken 500-ton vessel.

The concert and assembly hall in the former church of St James the Less was opened by the Duke of Kent in July.

1985

$400m. treasure found in galleon off Florida.
Hooliganism bans UK from European football.

The Gaumont cinema closed in January, a victim of the video boom and the growth of the finance industry. The building was demolished later in the year to be replaced by a bank building.

The new Lt-Governor, Sir Alexander Boswell, was sworn in during October to replace Sir Peter Le Cheminant.

Space shuttle Challenger explodes after launch. Liechtenstein allows women the vote.

1986

167

The massive £16m. North beach reclamation scheme starts to take shape as millions of tons of harbour bed silt were sucked up and pumped over the White Rock to create a huge parking area and the basis for the Queen Elizabeth II Marina. The huge civil engineering exercise was carried out with few hitches.

The remains of a Roman trading vessel, uncovered in the silt of the harbour bed during dredging, was lifted from the water and transferred to preservation tanks. The wreck was later nicknamed Asterix.

1986

Clint Eastwood becomes mayor of Carmel, California. US bombs Libya. Nuclear meltdown at Chernobyl, Russia.

Guernsey hit the international headlines when Gerald and Yvonne Gillow took the States Housing Authority to the European Court of Human Rights in Strasbourg after the UK Government acknowledged that the refusal of the authority to grant them a licence to live in the house they built in the Oberlands was a breach of their fundamental human rights.

The death knell of the Housing Authority offices which had stood on the Albert Pier for decades was sounded when the States agreed to spend £250,000 on refurbishing premises in Fountain Street for the authority. Housing Authority president Elizabeth Lincoln set the debate back on its heels when she announced that she had not asked to move and her staff were very happy at the Albert Pier. They did not want plush offices and would rather see the money spent on refurbishing States housing. But the States still agreed to the move and the building was later demolished.

Thousands of pounds worth of damage was caused when lifting gear on one of the harbour's heavy lift cranes failed while it was trying to lift the passenger catamaran Condor Kestrel. The lifting gear and hook crashed through the cat's superstructure. The crane driver escaped injury when the broken cable whiplashed back and smashed the crane cab's windows. The Board of Administration was cleared later of breaching factory safety laws on the grounds that the Harbour was not a 'factory'.

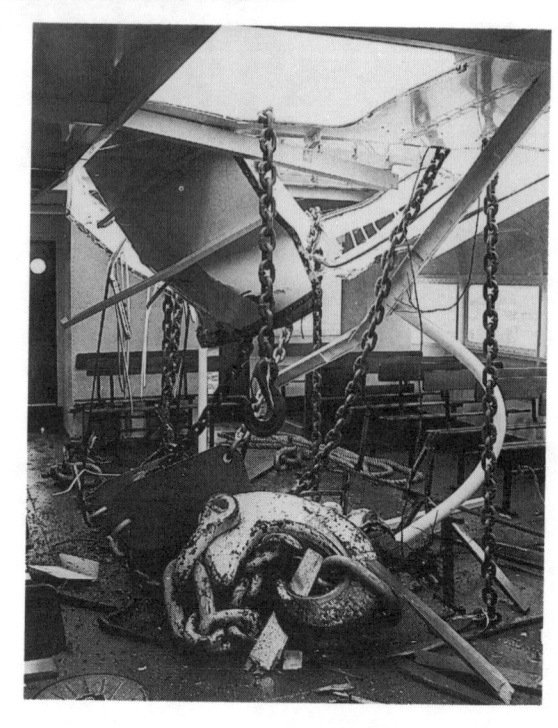

Phil Lynott of Thin Lizzie dies of overdose. Desmond Tutu enthroned as Archbishop of Cape Town, South Africa.

1986

Flaming June saw 1,270 runners start the biggest ever Hash House Harriers half marathon and 1,099 of them finishing the course. Aldershot's John Hood broke the tape in a second less than one hour eight minutes. Here the field sets off from the start at Pleinmont.

1986

Knighthood for Bob Geldof. Police and printers clash at Wapping.

There were grim faces as Sealink British Ferries and competitors Channel Island Ferries announced a merger that would mean the loss of 460 jobs. The National Union of Seamen crew took action immediately they received their redundancy notices and the Earl William blockaded the ro-ro ramp in St Peter Port Harbour. The ferry blockade became the central weapon in a nationwide dispute. It was 19 days before the union backed down and the blockade ended. Ship's officer Bill Roberts summed up by saying: 'There were no winners – only losers.' Sealink were eventually taken to court by Channel Island Ferries over control of the new hybrid company and CIF won.

Princess Anne paid a visit to the island in early May and delighted hundreds of islanders by her unscheduled walkabouts, chatting to many and receiving dozens of bunches of flowers. The visit culminated with a glittering ball at which hundreds of islanders were present.

Prince Edward made his first, and the island's second, royal visit of the year in spite of being unable to land because of fog. He travelled to Guernsey via Jersey and the launch Duchess of Normandy. While here he spoke to Grammar School pupils and attended a charity banquet at Beau Sejour.

1987

Zeebrugge ferry disaster. Hurricane hits Britain, Met Office blames computer.

Year of the hurricane. Gusts up to 110mph lashed Guernsey on 16 October, leaving a widespread trail of destruction. The winds were the strongest recorded in the British Isles that night and caused damage to properties, brought down trees and created turmoil for boatowners and the owners of this Cessna 172, which was flipped over, and this house at L'Eree which lost a gable. Most States Works Department men were called out to try to clear roads of fallen trees. During the storm the air pressure dropped to 962 millibars, just eight millibars above the lowest ever recorded in Guernsey back in 1872.

The hurricane damaged 246 acres of glasshouses and 17 acres were destroyed. They included these glasshouses at Pleinheaume.

172 **1987** Hitler's deputy, Rudolf Hess, dies in Spandau Prison, Berlin. 'Butcher of Lyon', SS commander Klaus Barbie, jailed for life.

Let the games begin: Sir Charles Frossard declares the second Island Games open to start six days of fierce competition involving more than 1,000 competitors from 17 islands, ranging from St Helena, 4,500 miles away in the South Atlantic, to Iceland. The Isle of Man emerged overall winner.

Nightmare on Wall Street as shares plummet. Young German Mathius Rust lands plane in Red Square, Moscow.

1987

173

What was the attraction and shouldn't they be looking over the sea wall? The answer was an impromptu pop concert by local band Splat who performed from the balcony of Cobo Bay Hotel.

Deep Freeze 87. The Model Yacht Pond was a shiny sheet of ice as the island was gripped by a particularly cold spell at the start of the year.

1987

Hungerford massacre – 14 die in Berkshire market town when gunman Michael Ryan goes berserk.

The dreaded Dutch elm disease strikes again. More than 100 infected trees a week were being felled in the summer of '87. Once felled they were taken to the rubbish tip at Bordeaux where they were turned into pulp (right).

The long and the short of it: Britain's tallest man, Chris Greener (left), all 7ft 6in. of him, was in Guernsey for the 42nd Liberation Day celebrations.

Mowing sand, are they mad? No, it is one of the many fun events staged each year at the Rocquaine Regatta (below).

SAS shoot three IRA in Gibraltar. Pound coin replaces note in UK. Eight-year Iran-Iraq war ends.

1988

A new day, a new law. At midnight on 1 July the wearing of seatbelts in the front seats of cars became compulsory (right), with an exception being made for taxi drivers. On day one of the new regulation it was thought that only two thirds of island motorists belted up, the rest choosing to ignore the law or claiming they simply did not know it existed!

Cardinal Basil Hume meets sixth form pupils from Blanchelande College during a visit to the island.

1988

Turin Shroud declared a forgery. One hundred thousand die in Armenian earthquake.

St Peter Port harbour and town front was 'transferred' to London and Earl's Court for the 34th International Boat Show sponsored by the Guernsey Tourist Board. The famous arena was transformed into a stylish replica of St Peter Port with brightly painted buildings of a Guernsey-French architectural style surrounding the central pool area.

The fury of the sea: gales lashed the island in January of this year and sheets of water fly into the air driven by force 11 winds.

Iraq uses poison gas on Kurds. First Boston gathering of people 'abducted by aliens'.

1988

A rare Siam Cup triumph: Martin Petit is chaired from the field after Guernsey's 12-8 win in Jersey, their first in 21 years of the annual inter-insular rugby competition.

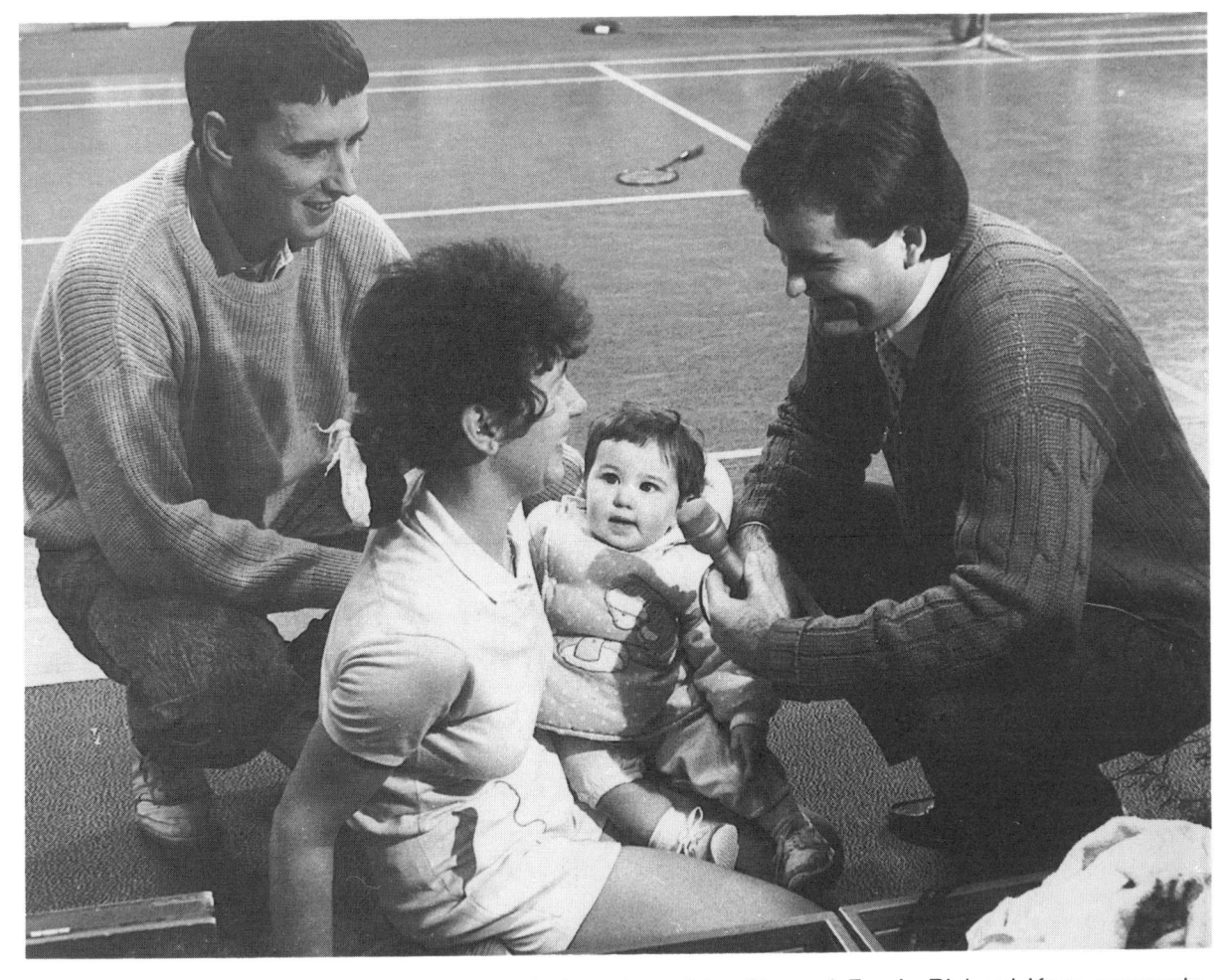

'We're proud of you mum.' Sally Podger is interviewed by Channel Four's Richard Keys moments after becoming the first mother to win the English badminton title. Looking on is baby Nicola and dad Andrew.

1988

Pan Am jumbo crashes at Lockerbie after bomb goes off in hold. Piper Alpha oil rig fire in North sea - 166 die.

Harvesting the publicity: Richard Ridout (right) and Dave Corson plough through some of the many magazines which carried stories on the 1988 Powerboat Championships. The annual powerboat week was a political hot potato within the island for many years.

As States Works Department teams worked throughout the day to clear flash floods – 1in. fell in six hours – Castel shopkeeper Dave Barrett (right) was shocked to be confronted with an eel swimming towards him. It turned out that the freshwater eel had appeared through an overflowing culvert near Saumarez Park.

Dictator Idi Amin is expelled from Uganda.
Ronald Reagan retires as US president.
Soviet army quits Afghanistan.

1989

Palm Sad-day! Vauvert was closed while a 100-year-old palm tree was craned away. The landmark palm was killed by the 1987 frosts.

Death Valley, St Saviour's? Parts of the reservoir looked more like a desert in the summer of 1989 as water levels dropped worryingly low.

1989

Berlin Wall comes down. Violent storms and updraughts lead to rain of sardines in Australia. Satellite Sky TV is launched.

A hero returns. Forty-eight hours after becoming the first Briton ever to win the World Women's Squash Championship, Martine Le Moignan flew into Guernsey. Among the large welcoming party for the 26-year-old former Blanchelande College girl was States Recreation president John de Putron.

Water restrictions hit everywhere in the summer of '89, including the Elizabeth College playing field at King's Road where assistant groundsman Tim Coulson was forced into watering the cricket square by hand!

They say he's soft at heart and England soccer star Paul Gascoigne did nothing to disprove the claim while on a visit to the island with Tottenham Hotspur. Here Gascoigne and Tottenham teammate Paul Walsh give local Gateway Club member Lawson Charlesworth a hug the young Spurs supporter will never forget.

Exxon Valdez grounds, releasing huge oil spill in Alaska. First elections in Russia since the 1917 revolution.

1989

181

Her Majesty goes walkabout through St Peter Port accompanied by Prince Philip, the Bailiff, Sir Charles Frossard, and the Lt-Governor, Sir Alexander Boswell. Thousands of islanders turned out to see Queen Elizabeth on her third visit to the island as sovereign and fourth all told. Before moving on to Alderney and Sark, Her Majesty toured the island and officially opened the Queen Elizabeth II Marina.

1989

Tienanmen Square massacre in Peking as army ends huge protests. Ninety six soccer fans crushed to death at Hillsborough.

Sports people abroad: Owen Le Vallee adresses the crowd on behalf of the Guernsey team at the opening ceremony of the third Island Games in the Faroes where the Sarnians placed fifth.

A World Champion for Guernsey. Local powerboater Donna James (right) and Tracie Clark celebrate winning the World Class Three 2-litre Championship in Guernsey waters.

Japanese dairy farmers admire two of the cows from Mike Gaudion's Maple Leaf herd. The Oriental contingent left Guernsey very impressed with the cows' high milk yield and high fat and protein content.

Furious East Germans plunder secret police records in Berlin. Nelson Mandela freed from prison.

1990

Adrian Breton (left), the silver medallist in 1986, won the Commonwealth Games gold medal for rapid fire pistol shooting in Auckland at the end of January. His score of 583 ex 600 was one better than runner-up Patrick Murray, of Australia.

Fleur Bougourd (right) won the women's world indoor bowls title in April when she beat Scot Elizabeth Wren by three sets to two in the final at the Guernsey Bowls Stadium at the Hougue du Pommier.

Guernsey hosted and won the inaugural European Cricketer Cup in May, beating Belgium in the final with the help of an unbeaten 99 by Paul Wakeford.

1990

Communist Party gives up power in Russia. Poll tax protest riots in Britain. Chile awakens from the Pinochet nightmare years.

Tektronix announced in the early days of January that it was to close its Guernsey operation in May and transfer the production and marketing facilities to Holland. The company helped its hundreds of staff find other employment and put the factory on the market for £7m. It was suggested that it could be used as States offices or a new airport terminal, but in March it was sold to Le Riche's for an undisclosed sum and they applied for permission to turn it into a supermarket.

The Napoleonic battery at Perelle, collapsed in March, one of the victims of a winter of storms which hit the island. Insurance companies assessed that the wind and the tide caused millions of pounds' worth of damage to many parts of Guernsey.

New York disco fire kills 87. Golfer Nick Faldo wins his second US Masters. Margaret Thatcher resigns. Queen Mother is 90.

1990

185

Condor 9, the company's first wavepiercing catamaran, arrived in August to start the service between the Channel Islands and Weymouth, but the high speed boat was hit by a series of problems and soon withdrawn from service.

The island celebrated the 45th anniversary of Liberation with a visit by Princess Alexandra.

1990

West and East Germany start to reunify.
First women ordained as Anglican priests.
Channel Tunnel drill holes meet.

The island's new Lt-Governor, Sir Michael Wilkins (above), arrived in the island in November on board HMS Guernsey. On arrival he and Lady Wilkins were greeted by the Bailiff, Sir Charles Frossard, and Lady Frossard.

In April Matt Le Tissier was named young player-of-the-year by his peers, the Professional Footballers Association. Two months later he married his childhood sweetheart, Cathy Loveridge.

The Right To Vote pressure group was formed in April by Mark Dorey and Dave Barrett to lobby for change in the way the island elects conseillers. It had immediate effect with the States agreeing the following month to review the island's constitution.

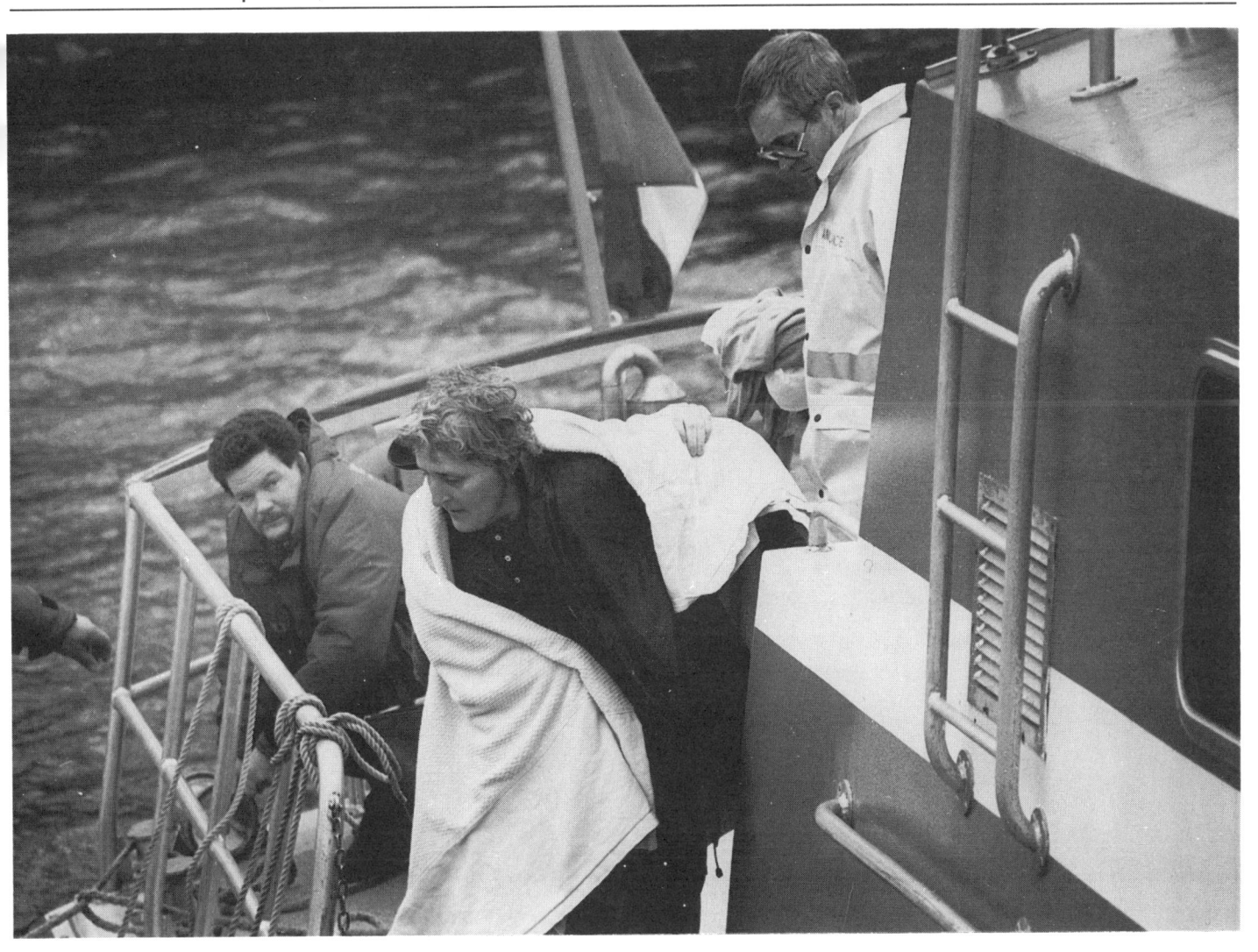

UN Operation Desert Storm ends Iraqi occupation of Kuwait, Saddam Hussein retains power, safe havens for Kurds.

1991

A Guernsey couple hit the headlines in March when, despite all the odds, they survived 18 hours adrift in a small wooden dinghy. Andre and Sylvia Lajoie (above) were described as 'lucky to be alive' by the skipper of the French lifeboat that had picked them up after their 19ft cabin cruiser, Assak, capsized in heavy seas off Sark. They were picked up some three miles west of Cap de Carteret following a massive air and sea search. Their two-metre folding dinghy (below) survived waves of up to 20ft during their ordeal, with the Lajoies using shoes to bail it out. A rescue services spokesman said the dinghy, which had been named The Dolly Bucket by its owners, was 'totally unsuitable for use as a lifeboat'. Following their nightmare, the Lajoies were brought to Guernsey by the lifeboat from Goury in France, and following checks at the Princess Elizabeth Hospital were allowed home to rest.

The Guernsey Zoo closed its doors in October after 30 years. In recent years it had eschewed larger animals in favour of smaller creatures that could be more easily catered for. But the rising costs of keeping animals to a high standard could not be met by a community the size of Guernsey, with a comparatively small number of visitors. Part of the problem was more regulations and demands being made on such establishments, said zoo director James Thomas.

1991

Nazi war criminals 'still living in Britain'.
Bangladesh cyclone kills 139,000, 10 million people left homeless.

Disposing of Guernsey's refuse, whether it be inert builders' waste or putrescible household rubbish, has always been a major problem. Making use of existing quarries is one solution, with land reclamation another. In January, work started on reclaiming land at Longue Hougue, St Sampson's (above), with the start of construction of a large enclosed area that would be filled with inert builders' refuse. The 27.8 acre site was first of all bounded by a stone wall, made using local stone and imported rock from France. The idea was to link the existing breakwater with rocky outcrops in the bay, and the work was expected to take about 67 weeks to complete.

Guernsey's reputation as a major financial centre received a boost when it was announced that top bank Credit Suisse was to create a prestigious development of offices and accommodation at Les Echelons, St Peter Port (left) - an area not formerly known for its outstanding aesthetics (unless you happened to be lucky enough to live in one of the houses overlooking the area which boasted spectacular views). Once the diggers moved in and cleared the Iron Stores and Channel Island Auto Spares buildings, the houses on the top of the hill looked rather exposed, and there was later some talk of problems being caused to their structure by the intensive work. But eventually all was resolved, and work on the construction of the offices proper got under way, with the building of one of the biggest scaffolding structures the island had ever seen.

Press baron Robert Maxwell drowns – millions missing from plundered pension funds. Freddie Mercury dies of Aids.

1991

After 50 years dominating the skyline at Chouet, one of the island's most distinctive landmarks finally crumbled into history in March. It had been inevitable that the German tower overlooking Ronez's Quarry would fall, but its collapse caught the workmen by surprise. They were eating their lunch in their work hut when they heard something fall outside. Rushing out, they saw the tower tremble, then collapse in a pile of concrete in the bottom of the quarry. Although the chances of its remaining above the quarry with so much intensive work going on below had been slim, there were those who were disappointed to see its demise - notably the island's historians and others interested in the Occupation and architecture.

1991

Yugoslavia disintegrates. Soviet Union replaced by Commonwealth of Independent States, president Gorbachev resigns.

Serious violent crime is, thankfully, rare in Guernsey, so when it occurs it seems doubly shocking. In early August, a young French woman was brutally attacked on cliffs near Soldiers' Bay in St Peter Port, and a search was mounted for her assailant that eventually encompassed the UK. Attack victim Laure Nicolas (18) was flown to Southampton General Hospital with severe head injuries, and for a time there was real concern about her condition. Fortunately, she recovered - although it was a long process, made even more frustrating when she was unable to be of much help to police in their inquiry. A description of the attacker was issued, and the BBC TV programme Crimewatch UK stepped in to film a recreation of the scene. But despite a number of leads, the perpetrator of what the police later described as attempted murder was not found.

Snow is always a big event in Guernsey, and it does not take much of it for the island to acquire something of a siege mentality. So when the temperature plummeted to a chilly -7.1C and islanders woke to find an inch of snow on their doorsteps, the schools closed, the snow chains came out, and large numbers of workers left their cars at home and ventured to their offices on foot. But it was not all fun and games, and firemen had to fight through the snow to reach the Savoy Hotel when fire broke out during the night of 7 February. Fortunately, despite the weather, they managed to bring the blaze under control in about half an hour. Some residents decided to give vent to their artistic abilities. Len Bretel and his son Peter came from a guitar-playing family, so rather than go for the traditional snow sculptures, the pair decided to create something a bit unusual.

Riots in Los Angeles leave 58 dead, 4,000 injured, 12,000 arrested after trial of police in Rodney King beating is abandoned.

1992

Blanchelande College's closure was announced in January. Last-ditch attempts were made by parents and local authorities to preserve the school but without success. The imposing south-coast building was left empty and offered for sale. The college has since reopened in Town.

A new Bailiff, Graham Dorey, took his oath of office on 19 February. The 800-year-old office saw him succeed Sir Charles Frossard. The ancient ceremony began in the Royal Court House and proceeded through the High Street to the Town Church. Sir Graham followed 70 others. He had worked as an advocate, people's deputy and law officer.

The craze for mountain biking prompted an outcry in January when it was reported that cliff paths were being destroyed by over-enthusiastic riders. Walkers were having to leap clear as the all-terrain cycles reached places normal bikes had never managed to negotiate. Steps, pedestrians and sharp corners proved no barrier and prompted the Board of Administration to warn that controls might have to be considered.

1992

Currency crisis rips European exchange rate mechanism apart – speculators win against central banks, making millions.

One of the island's premier hotels, the Royal, was damaged by fire on 2 June. Guests had to flee in their nightclothes and the night porter was taken to hospital suffering from smoke inhalation. Floodlights lit up the entire area just after 3am as the brigade tackled the blaze. It was the first of three mystery blazes which involved brigade members and police in hours of investigation. The hotel guests were taken to the St Pierre Park after the first fire which was brought under control in 40 minutes. Just six days later a second blaze erupted and two firemen were hurt. The brigade described the blaze as suspicious. No sooner was that shock ebbing than another fire ravaged the hotel on 28 June. There was serious damage to the empty building. Fire crews fought the blaze for two hours. Forensic tests failed to find a cause.

The perennial problem of transport costs became even more controversial in January. Cut-price packages were organised by the Guernsey Hotel and Tourism Association to try to bring people to the island in early season. Two nights accommodation for £46 was offered and a colour campaign in national newspapers was organised.

Mujaheddin topple president Najibullah's communist government in Afghanistan after 14 years of war.

1992

The appearance of the Val des Terres (above) changed drastically after Dutch elm disease forced the felling of the avenue of elms. Motorists were taken aback by the expansive view from the top of the road after the mature trees were gradually removed. A competition to landscape the area was launched and will replenish Les Terres. It was this year that the States abandoned the control policy for elm disease and had to accept that the situation was out of control. More than 500 affected elms were being reported each week and the clearance scheme ran out of funds.

The start of the spectacular floral Guernsey campaign which has 'greened up' much of the island was launched on 2 April (right). The Tourist Board enthusiastically announced plans to establish planted areas, organised garden competitions and encouraged people to grow more flowers. Flower baskets sprouted on lamp posts and circular displays appeared as if by magic in various parts of the Town as dedicated staff from States Works put into practice the ambitious idea. A heatwave in early summer led to staff using old quarry water and washing up water to preserve the precious displays.

1992

Pakistan admits having the Bomb. Bill Clinton becomes US president. Conservatives win fourth term. Famine threatens Somalia.

Outcry followed the news that Ebenezer Church was to close and possibly be demolished. Various ideas were floated to try to meet the £200,000 cost of repairs, including merging different congregations. Methodists decided that the old building needed to be demolished and replaced with an easy-to-maintain replacement, but public resistance and some swift political dealing led to its preservation.

A peal appeal was needed to ensure the Town Church bells could ring out for the imminent 50th Liberation. The Dean of Guernsey, the Very Rev. Jeffery Fenwick, called for the restoration. The Town's bells have been acclaimed as the finest in the Bailiwick but after a poor renovation project earlier this century and years of use, they needed some serious care. They were recast after a hugely successful appeal and a delicate operation in which tons of metal had to be gently moved in the close confines of the belfry. An attempt in 1736 to upgrade the bells went sadly wrong because the French firm employed to do the job had little or no knowledge of the finer points required to ensure its success. By the second half of the 19th century it was painfully obvious that they were far from well. On the King's birthday in 1913 the bells were rung for the last time. New ones were cast in France and their arrival was greeted with enthusiasm, but poor workmanship meant they could only be chimed rather than rung. Bell enthusiast Peter Gallienne spearheaded the 1992 appeal which successfully aimed to restore the St Peter Port bells to their former glory. A complete new bell frame was built together with all new frictional parts. The result was better than ever before.

Waco, Texas, siege ends in tragedy when FBI bungle assault, 72 die in resulting fire at Branch Davidian religious cult's ranch.

1993

First the embarrassment, then the pain. The 45ft Italian Class 1 offshore powerboat Cogeme-Iteco made front page news twice in the space of three days in the summer of 1993. The boat was left high and dry on rocks off Belle Greve Bay after a navigational faux pas as the crew acquainted themselves with local waters. Two days later the same boat overturned during the British Grand Prix having 'barrel-rolled' at high speed. Driver Francesco Pansini and co-driver Floriano Omoboni were rescued from their cockpit by St John Ambulance divers. Fortunately, neither man was seriously injured.

1993

Ruth Dreifuss elected to Swiss cabinet, 'a rare triumph over Swiss male chauvinism'. Commercial whaling plan rejected.

Thirty-nine French trawlers invaded St Peter Port to protest at Guernsey 'stealing' their fishing grounds at the Schole Bank. But the threatened blockade of the port was averted by skilful negotiation accompanied by helpings of locally caught fish and chips.

Quayside washout: Hundreds of islanders attracted to the town quay were left disappointed when the predicted 10.4m 'tide of the century' failed to materialise.

Rebellion suppressed in Moscow as tanks and troops clear the White House parliament building of dissidents.

1993

Around 4,000 islanders turned out on a fine spring afternoon to march along the east coast in protest at plans to reclaim and develop most of Belle Greve Bay. Their efforts were not wasted as the plans to fill in the bay were later dropped.

1993

Serbs and Croats at war, safe havens planned for Bosnians. Kim Campbell (46) is Canada's first woman prime minister.

The harbour boat Sarnia and an airport fire tender were called in to help firemen after the Norman Commodore caught fire en route from Guernsey to Portsmouth. Ten passengers were airlifted off the ferry by naval helicopters before the ship returned to St Peter Port. The battle against the blaze lasted through the night and into the next day, and at one stage there were fears that the ferry would sink at its berth.

New age travel: Condor 10, the first fast catamaran car carrier to serve the Channel Islands, arrives in St Peter Port after a 13,000 mile, 23-day journey from Tasmania.

Antarctic whale sanctuary is approved. Cuban boat people flee to USA. Smuggled plutonium is seized.

1994

White elephant of the year was the Emeraude Lines' 'high speed' ferry, Emeraude (above). This car and passenger carrier performed about as well as England's cricket team during the year. It suffered a series of technical problems and was eventually returned to the shipyard that built it. It was not the only high speed boating loss the island suffered. The organisers of the international power boat championships announced they were going to pull out of running them in Guernsey because of lack of support in the island. Islanders were divided over whether this was good or bad.

Shipping news hit the headlines in January when it was announced that Condor and Commodore Shipping have bought rival British Channel Island Ferries' passenger and freight business. This meant that 150 BCIF staff were to be made redundant, including 15 in Guernsey. News came later that BCIF lost £4m. in 1993. Here the Havelet (left) makes her last voyage in the BCIF livery.

1994

Amnesty International appeal for the rights of children. New International Tropical Timber Agreement to help the rainforests.

The historic first ever island-wide poll for conseillers saw the self-proclaimed 'man of the people' Eric Walters top the poll, with the support of 10,387 islanders. Runner up was Mike Torode with Ron Le Moignan third. The tiny margin of one vote separated Tony Bran and Jean Pritchard for the 12th place on the conseillers' bench and it took a recount to give Mrs Pritchard that honour. Former high flying politician Bob Chilcott's supporters were stunned when he failed to be elected, placing 17th of the 26 candidates.

The purchase of the lease of Lihou Island by the Board of Administration for £430,000 created a furore. Some States members thought that the money could have been better spent and others that the board should have consulted the House before laying out the cash. It seemed that the board were fearful that another owner could effectively close the island to visitors because the terms of the lease were unclear and visitation rights depended on the interpretation of where you could go to gather and dry seaweed on the island. The board did not have any definite plans for the 40-acre island with its open market house and priory ruins.

US lifts trade embargo against Vietnam.
Russian military try to defeat the Chechens.
ANC win election in South Africa.

1994

Picture of the year happened right in front of the camera lens of photographer Chris George, who was waiting to capture the Norman Commodore re-entering service after repairs to fire damage. But the ferry kept coming ... and coming. Chris kept snapping ... and snapping as the ferry ploughed into the Trident VI, reducing much of it to matchwood in seconds. No one was hurt and the Trident has been rebuilt, but Chris has a remarkable photo sequence.

The way Guernsey should mark the 50th anniversary of the Liberation caused much debate and many suggestions. The Liberation Day Committee's suggestion did not go down well with the public, or the States, and a new concept was called for. After the elections, a new committee came up with a design by Eric Snell, which pleased most.

1994

Whitewater scandal tarnishes President Clinton. Warning of food crisis in East Africa. North Korea agrees to nuclear inspections.

The recast Liberation peal of bells returned to the Town Church and were hung in the belfry.

50th anniversary of the liberation of Auschwitz from Nazi control – some 1,500,000 died there, 90% Jewish.

1995

A very wet winter saw the island become waterlogged, and when the rain persisted there were floods everywhere. The golf course on L'Ancresse Common was unplayable for many weeks. The scale of the problem is demonstrated by Ken Giles.

The first harbour ramp to handle roll-on, roll-off ferry traffic was detached from its mountings and loaded on to a barge in preparation for its journey to Holland after many years of service. It is being replaced by a new, bigger ramp.

1995

Mexico plunges into economic crisis. Pope visits Philippines and New Guinea. Spanish allowed to fish the 'Irish Box'.

Five patients at the Castel Hospital died of an influenza virus, many patients and staff were ill, and admissions to two wards halted in March while the cause of the illness was investigated.

It is 50 years since the end of the Occupation yet explosives from those days are still being discovered and destroyed. This one was blown up in a controlled explosion at Lihou Island.